Designing for
Bruges Flower Lace

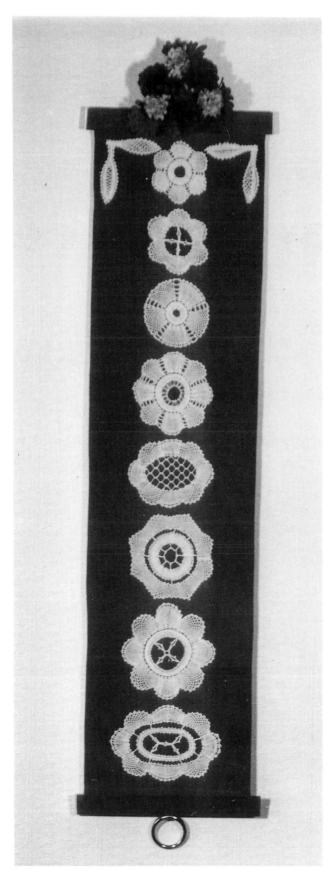

Frontispiece: Flower and Leaf Sampler

Designing for
Bruges Flower Lace

Edna Sutton

Dryad Press Ltd London

ACKNOWLEDGMENT

My sincere thanks to Eunice and Toos for their help with
reading the text, to Mary for her assistance with the
technical drawings, and to my husband who coached me
through the word processor and photographed all the
lace for this book.

ISBN 0 8521 9689 X

Typeset by Keyspools Ltd, Golborne, Lancs
and printed in Great Britain by
The Bath Press Ltd
Bath, Avon
for the publishers
Dryad Press Ltd
8 Cavendish Square
London W1M 0AJ

Contents

Introduction

Some of the basic techniques have been explained in my book *Bruges Flower Lace*, and reference should constantly be made to it with regard to their working. There is not sufficient space here to repeat all the techniques. A Glossary can be found in chapter 6.

The patterns designed for *Bruges Flower Lace* were of a simple nature, allowing the techniques to be practised and the skills perfected. Additional patterns have now been designed and some of the larger designs are included in this book. A chapter has been devoted to an explanation of how to produce a full-size pattern from a single section. More techniques have been introduced, based upon the traditional shapes used in this lace. There is a wide selection of patterns, some simple and others more advanced.

This book was written in the year of Halley's Comet's appearance, and the patterns are named after stars, planets and constellations extracted from astronomical references.

Modern coloured threads have been used to work selected pieces of lace, but they can be replaced by linen threads of the same thickness.

Some pieces of lace are too large for an individual to complete within a reasonable time. In these cases it is best if the project is undertaken by a group of lacemakers. Two of the articles in this book have been designed especially for group work. I hope you will enjoy working the designs and find the tasks interesting and rewarding.

ABBREVIATIONS

LH *left hand*
RH *right hand*
RS *right side*
WS *wrong side*
cl st *cloth stitch*
h st *half stitch*
d st *double stitch*
b st *back stitch*

Designing Bruges Flower lace

The word *lace* may be defined as the twisting, knotting, looping, plaiting and weaving of linen, cotton, silk, wool, and metallic threads. These techniques were used as far back as 5000 BC, and remnants of lace were found in Egyptian tombs.

The main areas where lace was made during the sixteenth and seventeenth centuries were Flanders and the Mediterranean region. From Flanders came Binche, Mechlin, Vlaanderse, Lille, Rosaline, Bruges, Duchesse and Valenciennes laces, and from the Mediterranean area came Venetian needlelace, all expensive items to purchase today. The techniques of one lace may be found in others; for example, Point de Paris in Binche lace, and small areas of needlelace known as Point de Gaze in Brussels lace. When looking at historical Brussels lace textiles, one can see the relationship between the Bruges Flower lace, coarse in texture, and the Brussels lace which is finer. Each lace contains flowers, leaves, scrolls, and fillings. One feature, 'three leaves', may be found in Bruges Flower lace, Duchesse, Brussels and Honiton lace.

The individual lace may be recognized by selecting from the following points:
a. yarn used, cotton, linen, silk. Fine medium or coarse in texture;
b. density of pattern, flowers, braids, scrolls, leaves, introduction of small areas of needle work, and the shape of the mesh used in the tulle ground;
c. ground stitches;
d. filling stitches;
e. use of double or single contour threads, to outline the different features used in the design;
f. picots, worked at the outer edge of the lace. These may be made by twisting two separate threads about the pin, or twisting the two threads together several times and then making the picot about the pin;
g. the shape of the textile, shawl, flounce, bertha, collar, fan, doily, yard lace, or a single motif.

Keeping the above points in mind, the following principles should be observed when designing Bruges Flower lace.
a. use a medium linen thread, 60/2. Finer cotton or linen threads may also be used to work this lace;
b. include flowers, leaves, scrolls and braids;
c. coarse fillings may be used to join these features together;
d. the piece of lace may be in the form of a doily, tray cloth, coffee cloth, collar, single motif, fan, mobile, or a household article.

With these points in mind, details are given to design a pattern and make a pricking for a square doily. The design will be simple, using basic shapes, simple stitches and techniques. Some of the prickings found in the book are larger than the page can accommodate. A quarter or half of the pricking will be given. The diagrams will show how the quadrants are joined together to make the whole pattern, and from this pattern the pricking will be made. Great care, accuracy, and precision are essential when making the pattern, thus ensuring a correct pricking.

The following equipment is required for this task:
a. drawing board;
b. pricking board;
c. a collection of draughtsman's tools;
d. good quality tracing paper;
e. a sheet of clear film;
f. pricking card;
g. ruler, set square, protractor and draughtsman's pins;
h. plain white drawing paper;
i. 3H and 6H drawing pencils;
j. a fine 'Rotring' pen;
k. a thick felt-tipped pen;
l. a fine felt-tipped pen.

PHOTO I A selection of equipment required to make
patterns and prickings

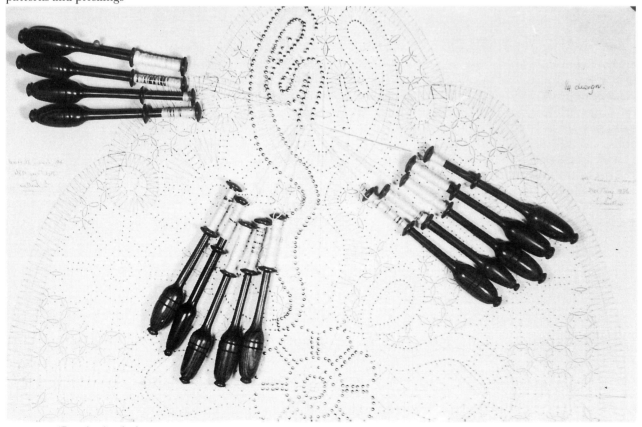

PHOTO 2 'Proving' a design

DESIGNING THE PATTERN

When old Bruges Flower lace patterns are examined, the simplicity of the design is obvious. Only one flower design is used, although its size is varied: one design of braid, where the stitch used may be varied at the discretion of the lacemaker; one leaf shape, where again the stitch used may be a personal choice. To join the features together, one or two fillings may be used.

Make several rough sketches by using a thick felt-tipped pen. Draw the features within the shape of the motif. Draw several motifs. Select the best; at this stage features may be altered and new ones added. Remember to keep the shape and the features simple and neat.

These principles will help you to decide which braid, flower, leaf, stitches, and filling to use.

Making the pattern

1. On a piece of tracing paper, and with a fine felt-tipped pen, mark the horizontal and vertical lines. The right angles will make one section or quadrant of the pattern. It may even be necessary to mark it into smaller sections, i.e. eighths.
2. Turn over the tracing paper and place it on a sheet of white drawing paper. Secure it at the top corners with draughtsman's pins on a drawing board.
3. Slide the selected sketch between the two layers of paper, so that the sketch lies within the quadrant. Using the 3H pencil, lightly trace the outer line of the design.
4. Starting with the flower in the centre, draw the inner circle line and the outer edge of the flower line, as shown in Fig 1.

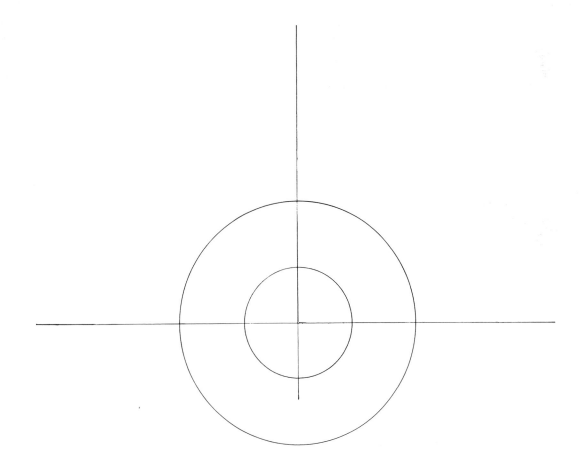

FIG 1 Inner circle line and outer edge of the flower line

FIG 2 Outer edge divided into six equal parts

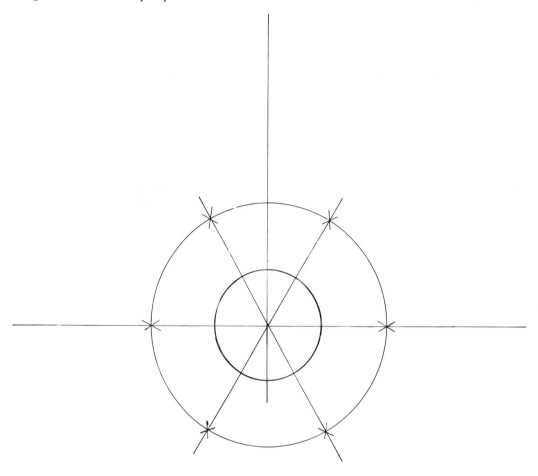

5. Divide the outer edge into six equal parts. This is done by using a pair of compasses set at the radius of the outer circle and then stepped round the outer circle. Consult Fig 2.

6. Draw the edge of the petal in the top RH quadrant. Mark the pinholes at the inner edge and then on the outer edge of the petal.

7. Put in the worker line and work out the position of b st if any are required. This is shown in Fig 4.

8. Mark out a 45-degree angle on the paper and draw a simple braid around the flower. Use a ruler and a sharp pencil to mark the width of the braid.

9. Extend the width of the braid where necessary, curving the braid within the area. Put in the worker lines, noting that the marks are closer together on the inner curve, and wider on the outer curve.

On the straight parts of a braid the pinholes are measured carefully with a ruler or a tracing wheel of the correct dimensions. The existing pinhole spacing already marked is suitable for 60/2 Bouc linen thread. Experience will show that the pinmarks are placed closer together to accommodate a finer thread.

The filling
1. Filling no. 3, plait-with-picots, has been chosen for this motif. Make a tracing of the filling on page 104, and use it to complete the pattern. It is important to keep the filling at the correct angle. Observe the diagram (Fig 5). Match the filling lines to correspond with the pinholes of the braid, flower, and leaves, etc. It is permissible in some cases to sew into the edge of the braid between the pinloops.

The edging
1. With the help of the diagram for the third plait-with-picot edging (Fig 60), mark in the edging carefully. Care must be taken to make a neat join where the braid dips in each part of the quadrant.

FIG 3 Petal planned in RH quadrant

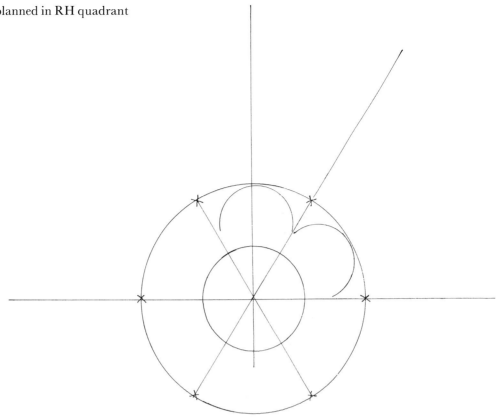

FIG 4 The petal completed in the RH quadrant

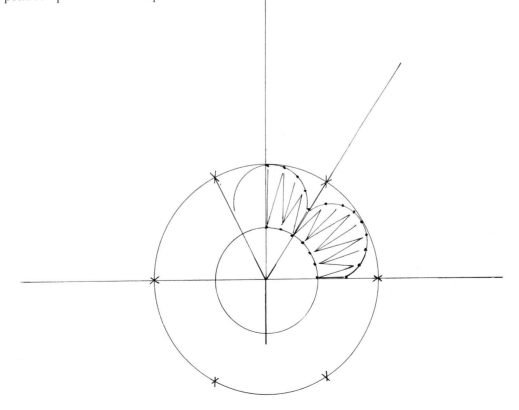

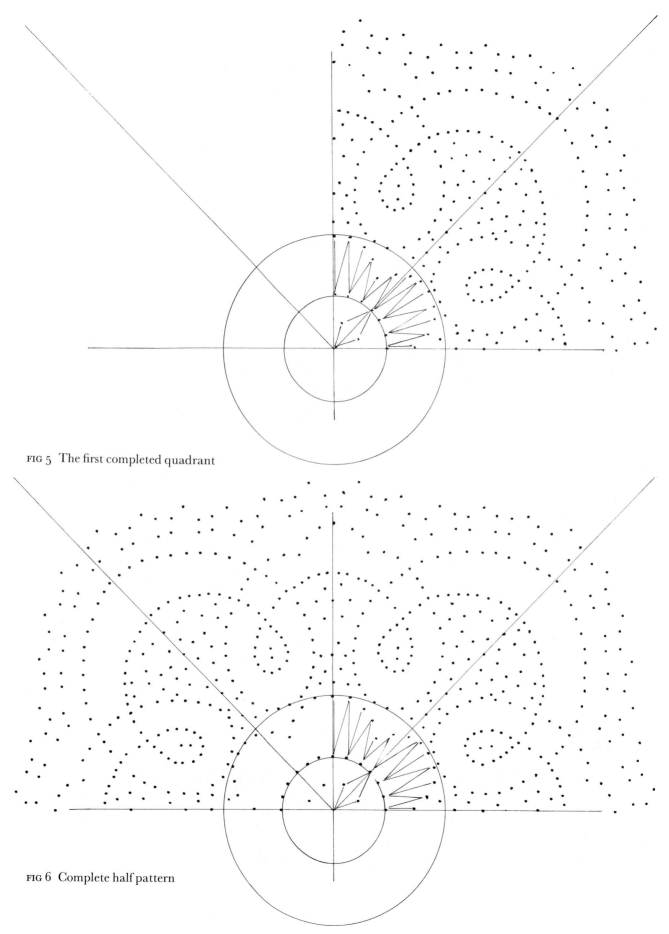

FIG 5 The first completed quadrant

FIG 6 Complete half pattern

Making the complete pattern

1. The quarter section, the first quadrant, of the pattern should now be pricked out on a piece of clear film.

2. Turn the film over and place it at the LH side of the first quadrant, already marked on a piece of tracing paper. Carefully match the pattern at the centre.

3. Prick out the second quadrant, and half of the pattern is now complete.

4. Reverse the quadrant pricking, and place it on the area for the third quadrant. Take care again to match the design. Accuracy is essential at this point. Prick out the third quadrant. Three quarters of the pattern are now complete.

5. Again reverse the quadrant pricking, and slide it into position, matching the design along two edges. Prick out. This completes the pattern.

6. Mark in the worker lines, not forgetting the b st, on flower, braid, edging, and the filling.

7. The pattern is now complete and ready for pricking out on a piece of card. All the worker lines should be transferred to the pricking and marked with a 'Rotring' pen. The pricking is now ready for use. The above points can be applied to produce new accurate prickings from well-used ones. Instructions follow for working this design.

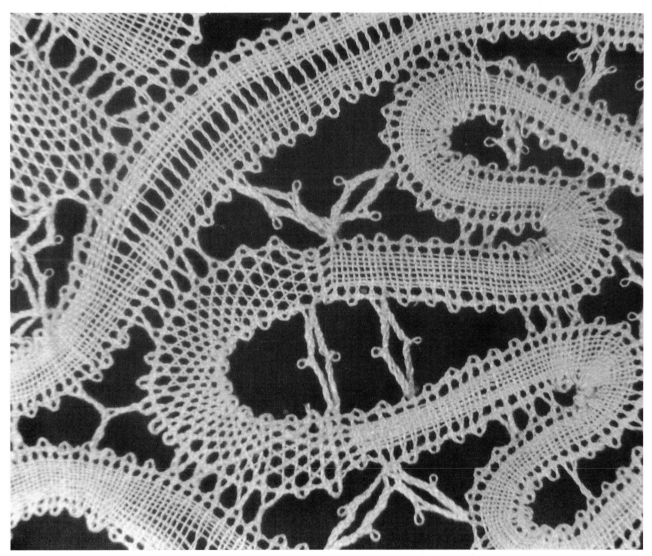

PHOTO 3 A selection of braids and alternative methods of joining braids

PHOTO 4 Details of
Flower 10, a double-stitch
braid and two centre
fillings

PHOTO 5 *Pegasus*

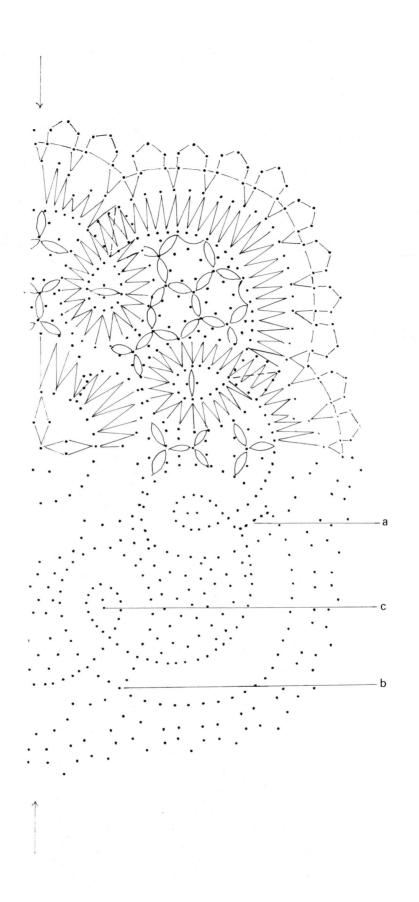

FIG 7 *Pegasus*

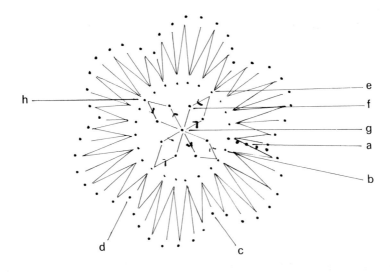

FIG 8 Pattern for flower no. 2

PEGASUS   Linen 60/2

Techniques used in working the motif—cl st, h st, d st, d st edge braid, plait-with-picot, joining into a circle, filling no. 3, edging no. 3, crossing two braids, flower no. 2.

Method of working the motif

1. Using the prepared pricking start by working the flower.
2. Along a line at *a* put up five pins and hang on two pairs of bobbins on each pin. Using the first pair start to work a row of cl st to the outer edge. Work the d st edge, remembering to twist the worker pair an extra time before putting up the pin.
3. When the d st edge has been worked at *b*, return in cl st to the inner edge. Work the d st edge, and note that when returning to this pinhole for a second time, a b st is worked. Work the b st and return to the outer edge in either cl st or h st whichever you have chosen to work. Firm and shape the passive threads to follow the outer curve of the petal. When *c* has been worked, separate the petals with a row of d st, worked towards the inner edge.
4. Work the second petal in either cl st or h st. When the pinhole at *d* has been worked, separate the petals again with a row of d st worked from the outer to the inner edge.

5. Continue to work the petals, stopping at *e* in the last one. The centre filling can be worked in the following way before the last petal is completed.
   The filling is worked in an anti-clockwise direction.
i. At *e* work a d st and put up a pin.
ii. Work a plait to *f* with the two edge pairs. Work a picot. Continue the plait to *g*. Put up a pin between the pairs. A twist is already on each pair when working a h st plait.
iii. Work a plait-with-picot to *h*. Take out the pin at *h* and sew in the LH pair. Then pass the other pair through the loop in the direction you are working. Replace the pin. Firm the threads. Continue to work the plait-with-picot back to *g*.
iv. Place the pairs about the pin again.
v. Work the other groups of plaits-with-picots by following the arrowed lines until *g* is worked for the last time. Remove the pin at *g* and sew through all the loops about the pin. Slide the other pair through the loop. Put the pin back into the hole, untwist the threads and firm them. Complete the last plait-with-picot to *e*. Sew in the RH pair and slide the other pair through the loop. Work a d st to bring the two pairs back into the petal. Finish the petal, and work a row of d st to the inner edge. Join the threads into their corresponding pinloops. Tie off and cut the threads close to the lace.

The braid

1. Along the line at *a* put up five pins. Hang two pairs of bobbins on each pin.
2. Using h st, work the section of braid, noting where the b st are worked.
3. At *b* change to cl st and note that b st are worked in order to accommodate the curve of the braid.
4. At *c* work the plait-with-picot, using the two edge pairs. Work the top one first (anti-clockwise direction). Two sewings are made into the petal. Finish the cl st part of the braid.
5. Cross the braid.
6. The next section is worked in h st.
7. Complete the braid in this sequence, remembering:
a. the sewings;
b. crossing the braids;
c. the plait-with-picots in the braid loops.
8. At *a* the starter pins must be removed to allow the braid to be worked. Replace the pins so that the braid may be joined.

The filling

Using filling no. 3, work each section carefully.

The edging

Edging no. 3 was used to outline this motif.

PHOTO 6 A quadrant of *Pegasus*

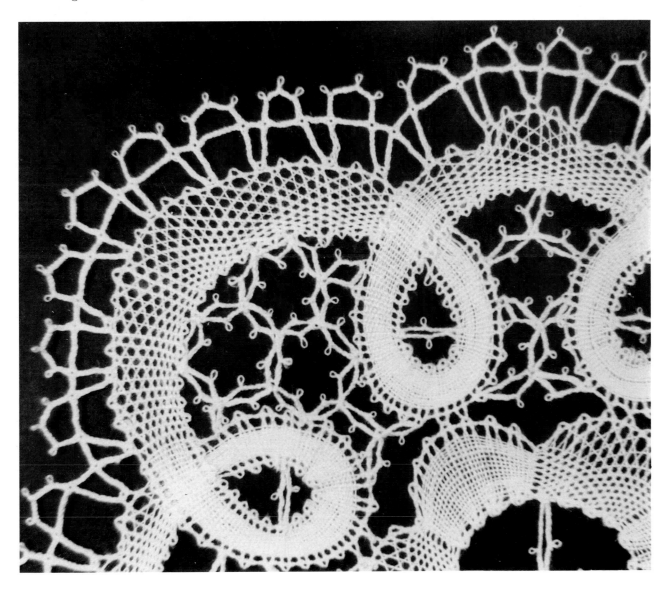

PHOTO 7 Doily 28cm in diameter, designed and worked by
the author.

Chapter Two

Further techniques in Bruges Flower lace

There are several techniques which still need to be described; fillings, braids, and flowers. In my first book, *Bruges Flower Lace*, four fillings were selected and an additional three will be described here. The first two will complete a set of six glass-mats, and the third one has been used in an edging for a dinner mat in chapter 5.

CAPPELLA   Linen 60/2   filling no. 5

This motif introduces a simple filling, using 48 bobbins. It should be worked carefully and accurately. The same number of plait stitches should be used in each plait. When each plait is worked, put up a pin between the pairs. Push the pin down and leave the plait until ready for joining with the worker plait. Do not plait too tightly.

Techniques used in working the motif—d st edge braid, h st, joining into a circle, tying off several threads, plaits, plait-with-picot, edging no. 1, sewings into a pinloop.

Method of working the motif

1. Prepare the pricking as described on page 107.
2. Along a line at *a* put up five pins. Hang two pairs of bobbins on each pin, side by side.
3. Work a d st with the first two pairs. Using h st work to the outer edge. Work a d st edge.
4. Complete the braid, using h st, and work a d st edge at both inner and outer edges.
5. Join the braid into a circle. Sew one pair into a pinloop made about the starter pin.
6. Tie off all the threads as explained on page 112.

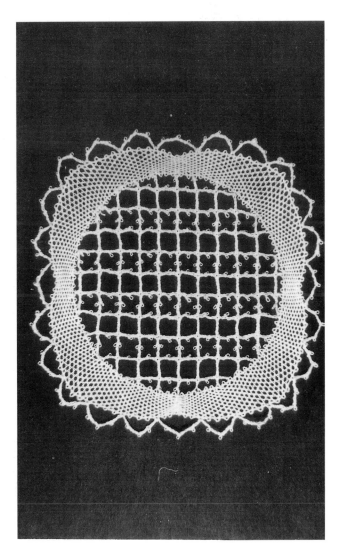

PHOTO 8 *Cappella*, filling no. 5

The filling

Make sure that sufficient thread is wound on to the empty bobbins so as to avoid joining a thread in the middle of a plait.

1. Sew in two pairs of bobbins, one pair at a time, into the pinloops at *c* and *d*, and four pairs at *e*.
2. Working from right to left, work the plait-with-picot, plait and the plait-with-picot to *b*, joining the plaits with a windmill join.
3. Sew these two pairs into the pinloop at *b*. Leave the pairs hanging as passive pairs.
4. Sew in pairs as required to act as passive and worker pairs. The filling may be worked from right to left, sewing out the worker pairs.
5. Remember to put up a pin between the pairs to support the plait.
6. As the filling progresses, the rows will terminate. The pairs must be sewn out—do not tie off. When all the sewings are complete, inspect the filling and make any necessary corrections. One or two plaits may be out of line, and a quick unpick and re-sew will correct any errors.
7. The pairs may now be tied off in reef knots. Carefully cut off the threads close to the knots.

The edging

Work edging no. 1 around the outline of the motif.

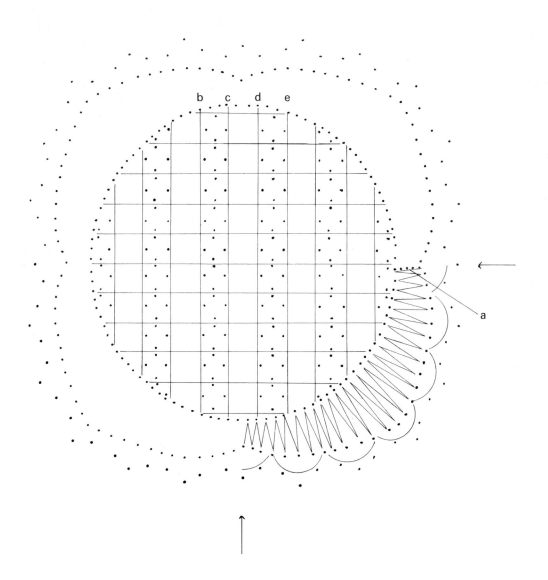

FIG 9 *Cappella*, filling no. 5

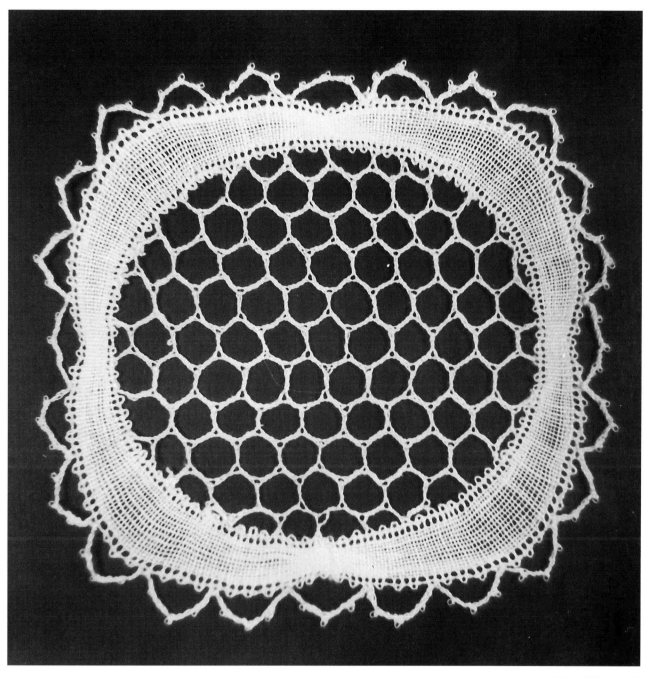

PHOTO 9 *Vega*, filling no. 6

VEGA Linen 60/2 filling no. 6

This filling is worked using plaits and false plaits. The rows are worked left (L) to right (R) and right to left whenever possible, and joined to the row above with false plaits. Two pairs of bobbins are used to work this filling, remembering to keep the threads in use as long as possible to avoid unnecessary joining of the threads. The pairs may be sewn into the small bar under the pinhead, plaited, and sewn again in a similar way where needed. The plait will not be seen from the RS.

Techniques used in working the motif—cl st, d st edge braid, sewings into a pinloop, plaits, false plaits, plait-with-picot, edging no. 1, joining the braid into a circle, tying off several threads.

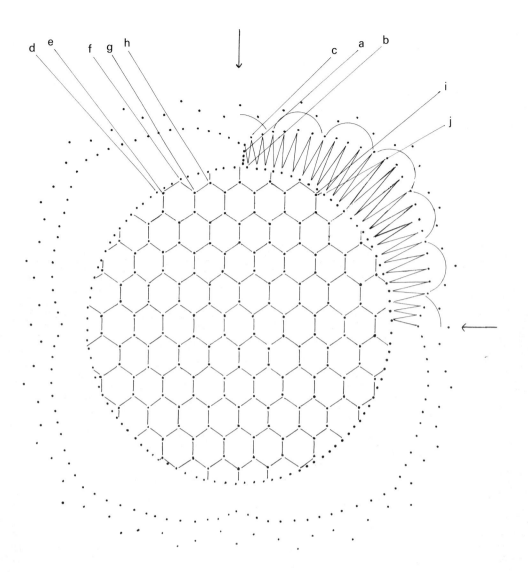

FIG 10 *Vega*, filling no. 6

Method of working the motif

1. Prepare the pricking as described on page 107.
2. Along the line at *a* put up five pins. Hang two pairs of bobbins on each pin, side by side.
3. At the inner edge work a d st with the first two pairs at *b*. Using cl st work towards the outer edge and work the d st edge at *c*.
4. Continue working the d st edge braid. Take care to follow the shape of the outer edge, by shaping the passive threads. After each row has been worked, firm these passive threads. Good, even tension is essential, especially at the widest and narrowest sections.
5. Join the d st edge braid into a circle and tie off the threads in the usual manner. Cut off the threads close to the lace.

The filling

1. At the pinloop at *d*, sew in two pairs of bobbins. Work one h st of the plait. Put up a pin between the pairs at *e*. Make one twist with each pair.
2. Work a short plait and sew into the pinloop at *f*.
3. Work the plait to *g*. Put up a pin. Work a further plait to *h*. Work a false plait sewing into the pinloop of the braid.
4. Complete the row of plaits and false plaits. When the last sewing at *i* has been worked, make a plait and sew into the small bar under the pinhead at *j*. Tie and cut off. Working from L to R work the second row of plaits and false plaits.
5. Complete the filling, remembering to avoid tying and cutting off the threads unnecessarily.

BRAIDS

Bruges Flower lace is a 'piece' lace, round, oval, square, rectangular or occasionally triangular in shape. To enable more interest to be given to the braid framing the flowers, leaves, and other features, sections of the braid may be curved. Each section may be broken by small horizontal plaits, or decorated with small holes. The braids are worked with a d st edge, using cl st or h st.

PHOTO 10 *Rigel*, braid with a hole

RIGEL   Linen 60/2

Rigel was designed to use two of the new techniques described in this chapter, braid with a hole and filling no. 6.

Techniques used in working the motif—cl st, h st, d st edge braid, crossing of two braids, sewing into a pin loop, braid with a hole, h st bud (filling no. 2), filling no. 6, joining into a circle, tying off several threads.

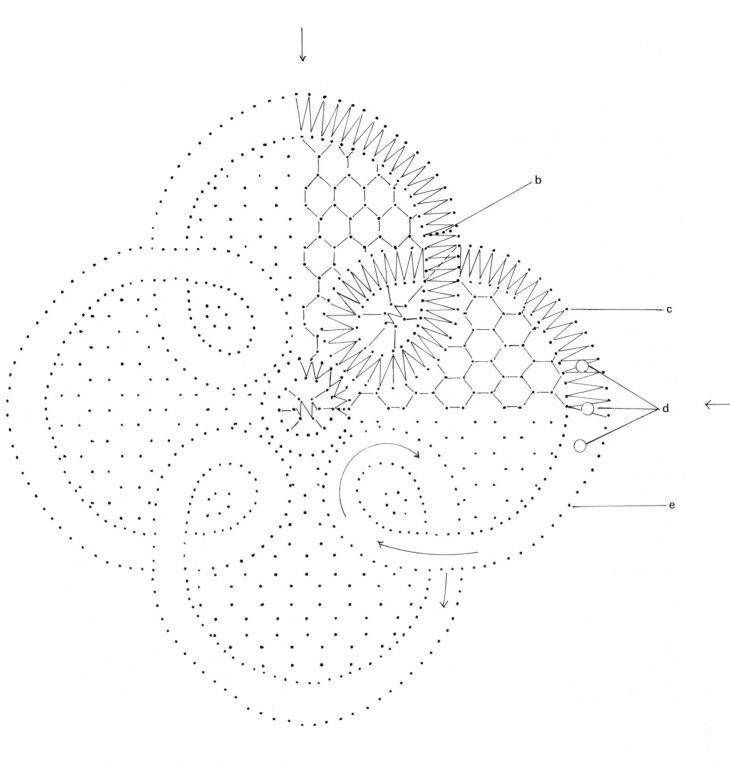

FIG 11 *Rigel*, introducing 'a hole in the braid'

FIG 12 Quarter section of the inner circle

Method of working the motif

1. Prepare the pricking as explained on page 107.
2. Along the line at *a* put up four pins. Hang two pairs of bobbins on the first and last pins, side by side, and one pair on each of the other pins.
3. Start by working a d st with the two pairs on the first pin, at the inner edge. Using cl st work towards the outer edge, where a d st edge is worked. Note where the b st are worked and complete the circle.
4. Join the circle by sewing one pair into one starter pinloop about the pin. Take care to avoid disfiguring the first pinloops at the outer and inner edges. Tie off the threads in the usual way.
5. Along a line at *b* put up five pins. Hang two pairs of bobbins on each pin, side by side.
6. Take the first two pairs at the inner edge and work a d st. Using h st work towards the outer edge and work the d st edge.
7. Work the h st braid in a clock-wise direction. Sewings must be made into the edge of the small circle. Cross the braids. When the pin at *c* has been worked, work a row of d st towards the inner edge. The stitch will change to cl st.
8. Consult the photograph (Fig 11) and work the braid until *d* is reached at the inner edge. Work the edge stitch and cl st through three pairs. Allow the worker pair to hang as a passive pair. Take up the next passive pair and use it as a new worker pair. Cl st to the outer edge and work the edge stitch. Work a few more rows of cl st.
9. Work two more holes in the braid where marked, and finish working the small area of cl st braid. At *e* work a row of d st to the inner edge. The stitch now changes to h st.
10. Complete the braid, making the sewings into the edge of the small circle. Note the b st, the change of stitch, the holes in the braid, and the correct crossing of the braids.
11. Join the braid into a circle, avoiding any disfiguration of the first inner and outer pinloops. Tie and cut off the threads close to the lace.

Filling no. 2

1. Work the h st bud in the centre of the small circle and braid loops.

Filling no. 6

1. Work filling no. 6 in the large areas, paying particular attention to the small plaits and false plaits of each area. Omitting these will disfigure the filling and mar the appearance of the motif. Continue using the threads, avoiding any unnecessary cut-offs and new joins.
2. Examine the filling and note that the sections are symmetrical and all the pinholes of the filling have been used.

JUPITER   Linen 60/2

The second motif resembles a large flower. Each section of the braid is divided by a row of d st. Some of the traditional patterns are outlined with a plait-and-picot edging. The braid frames a flower with eight petals which are attached to the inner circle using the raised edge technique. A plait-with-picot filling joins the braid and flower together.

Techniques used in working the motif—cl st, h st, d st edge braid, b st, raised edge sewings, plait-with-picot, sewings, joining into a circle, filling no. 3, flower no. 5.

Method of working the motif

The flower
The inner circle
1. Prepare the pricking as described on page 107.
2. Along the line at *a* put up four pins and hang on eight pairs of bobbins, side by side. Using the last two RH pairs of bobbins work a cl st. Twist each pair twice and put up a pin to the left of both pairs. A 'four-about-the-pin' edge (straight edge) is worked here.
3. Cl st to the inner edge where a d st edge is worked.
4. Complete the inner circle in cl st, using the four-about-the-pin edge at the outer edge and a d st edge at the inner edge.
5. At *b* start to work the filling, using the two edge pairs. The filling is worked in an anti-clockwise direction. Remember to make a sewing through the pinloops at each of the four centre pins.
6. Finish working the inner circle and join the circle in the usual way. Place one pair of bobbins, at the outer edge, to one side for use in the petals. Cut off the other threads close to the lace.

The petals
1. Along the line at *c* put up five pins and hang on ten pairs of bobbins.
2. Using the pair from the inner circle as workers, work a row of cl st to the outer edge. Work a d st edge and return to the inner edge, using cl st.
3. Make a sewing, using the first bar of the first pinloop. All the bars will be used for sewings to work the raised edge. Instead of twisting the workers before making a sewing, cross the workers once. This

PHOTO 11 *Jupiter*, braid divided with a row of double stitches

will bring the threads closer to the raised edge. When using h st take the threads as they come.

4. Finish working the petals in the stitch of your choice remembering to work the last row of d st and join the first and the last petals together by sewing the threads into the loops about the starter pins. Tie off in the usual way. Cut the threads close to the lace.

The braid

1. Along the line at *d* put up five pins and hang on ten pairs of bobbins, side by side.

2. Using the first LH pair work a d st and start to work the braid in cl st towards the outer edge. Work the d st edge and continue working the braid until *e* is reached. Note the b st in the centre of each section.

3. At *e* start to work the plait-with-picot filling in an

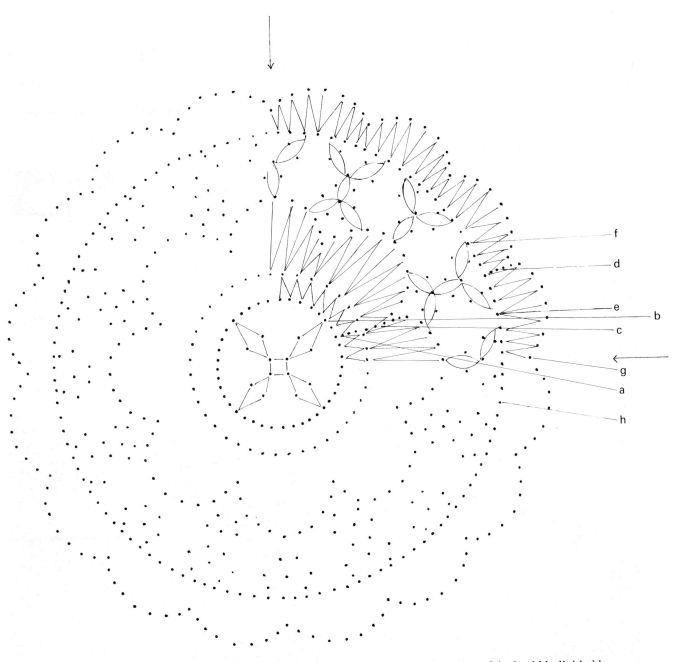

FIG 13 *Jupiter*, each section of the braid is divided by a row of double stitches

anti-clockwise direction. Two sewings are made into the pinloops of the flower. At *f* a pin is put up between the two pairs and left. As the braid is completed a sewing is made into this pinloop.

4. Complete the section of the braid. At *g* work a row of d st from the outer to the inner edge.

5. The next section is worked in h st and at *h* work the next part of the plait-with-picot filling, in an anti-clockwise direction. The first sewing is worked into the pinloop of the braid and the second one worked into the pinloop at the centre of the petal. Finally work the last sewing into the pinloop of the braid.

6. Complete the braid in this manner, working the plait-with-picot filling as it progresses. Make a sewing into the pinloop of the first part of the filling at *f*.

7. Join the braid into a circle in the usual manner. Tie off the threads carefully. Cut the threads close to the lace.

MARS Linen 60/2

This motif was designed to introduce another braid. This braid is very similar to the petals used in the flowers. In the design the petals of the flower and the curved edge of the braid are both attached to an inner circle by means of a raised edge.

Techniques used in working the motif—cl st, h st, d st edge, four-about-the-pin edge, d st plaits, b st, raised edge sewings, joining into a circle, a tally, Dieppe ground, tying off threads.

Method of working the motif

Inner circle

1. Prepare the pricking as described on page 107.
2. Along the line at *a* put up four pins and hang on six pairs of bobbins.
3. Starting at *b* work a cl st. Make two twists on each pair. Using cl st work towards the inner edge. At *c* work a d st edge. Return to the outer edge where a four-about-the-pin edge is worked.
4. Complete the inner circle in this way, working a b st at each pin of the inner edge.
5. Join the threads into a circle, sewing one pair into one pinloop made about the pin. Firm the threads and tie them off in the usual manner. Lay one pair at the outer edge, to the back of the work, to be used to work the petals. Cut off the other threads close to the lace.

The petals

1. Along the line at *d* put up four pins. On the LH pin hang on one pair of bobbins, and two pairs on the other three pins. Bring the pair from the inner circle and place these threads on the first pin. Twist each pair once. Work a row of d st towards the inner edge.
2. Make a sewing at *e*, using both bars for this sewing, and each bar of the next three pins, and both bars at the fifth pin. When using cl st cross each pair once and use the LH thread to make the sewing, passing the RH thread through the loop.
3. Finish each petal by twisting each pair once and work a row of d st to the outer edge.
4. Divide the pairs and work the small plaits to the corresponding pinholes of the next flower. Put up the pins between the pairs of each plait.
5. Work a row of d st from the outer to the inner edge. Make the sewing as before.
6. Work all the petals and when the last pin has been put up at *f*, work the small plaits and sew each pair into the corresponding pinloops. Tie off each pair in a reef knot and cut the threads close to the lace. Work the tally.

The braid

The inner circle

1. Along the line at *g* put up four pins and hang on six pairs of bobbins. Work the inner circle of this braid as described for the inner circle of the flower. Join the braid into a circle, and tie the threads. Place one pair from the outer edge to the back of the work. This pair will be used to work the outer circle.

The outer circle

1. Along the line at *h* put up four pins and follow the instructions given for the petals of the flower. Notice that no b st will be worked as both bars will be used for each sewing.

The filling

Dieppe ground is used in the motif. Sew in pairs above the pinholes at the top of the motif, adding pairs as required and sewing out pairs when no longer needed.

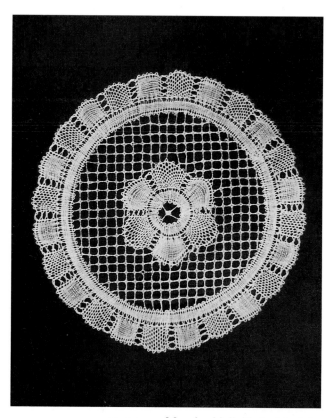

PHOTO 12 *Mars*, braid divided with plaits

FIG 14 *Mars*, the outer braid is similar in shape to the
petals of the flower

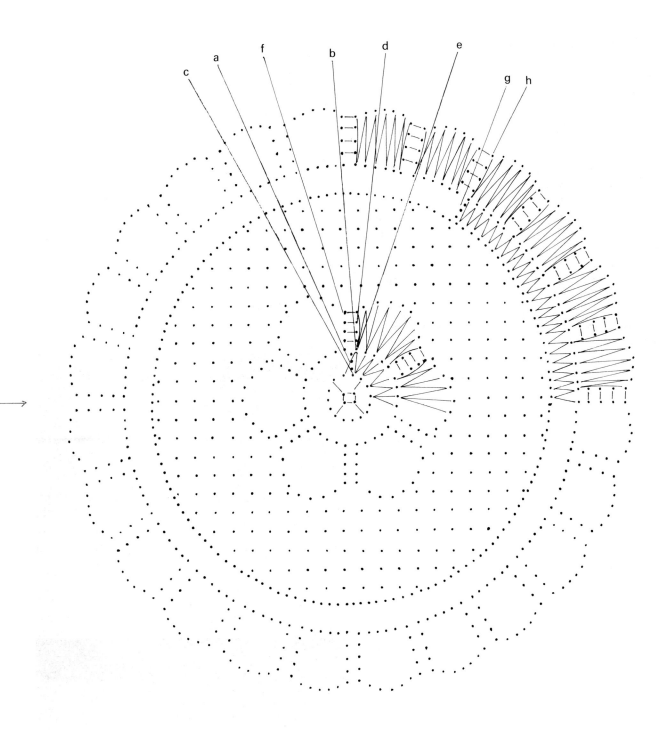

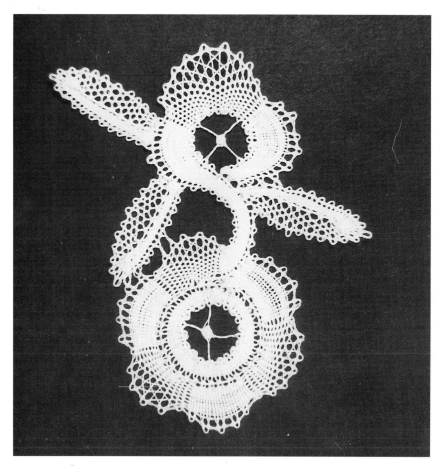

PHOTO 13 *Gemma*

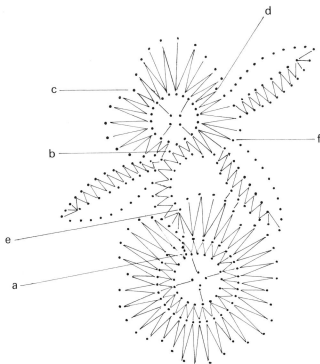

FIG 15 *Gemma*, a small motif introducing three more techniques

30

GEMMA   Tanne thread no. 30

In chapter 5 you will see a design of a basket of flowers. It utilizes several techniques found in this lace. As you will see, the motif has been adapted to include three of these techniques, a new flower shape, joining two flowers with a stem, and a broken spider.

Techniques used in working the motif—cl st, h st, four-about-the-pin edge, a tally, sewing into a pinloop, b st, a false plait, a leaf with a raised vein, d st edge, joining into a circle, tying off several threads, a raised edge, flower no. 3, a broken spider.

Method of working the motif

1. Prepare the pricking as explained on page 107.
2. Start to work the motif with the inner circle of the large flower.
3. Along a line at *a* put up three pins. Hang two pairs of bobbins on each pin. At the outer edge work a cl st with two twists on each pair, put up a pin to the left of these pairs.

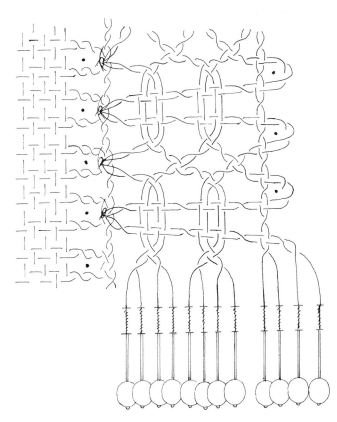

4. Using cl st work towards the inner edge, where a d st edge is worked. Complete the inner circle, working a four-about-the-pin edge (straight edge) at the outer edge and a d st edge at the inner edge. Note the b st. Firm the threads carefully.
5. Join the braid into a circle in the usual way. Tie off the threads. Place one of the threads near the outer edge to the back of the work. Cut off the other threads close to the lace, and leave the circle.
6. Along the line at *b* put up three pins. Hang on nine pairs of bobbins.
7. Observe the photograph of the motif (Photo 13). You will notice that the petals are worked alternately in cl st and h st. Each petal is separated by a row of d st, worked from the outer to the inner edge, *c* and *d*.
8. Using cl st start to work the first petal from the inner to the outer edge. Note the b st.
9. The last of the three petals is worked in cl st, and continues into the stem and along into the large flower using a d st edge. Firm and shape the passive threads and note the b st. Make a sewing through the b st, at *e*.
10. The petals of the large flower are worked alternately in cl st and h st. Each petal is separated with a row of d st. Sewings must be made into the inner circle of the large flower, to complete the raised edge. Follow the worker line carefully and notice which bars must be used.
11. Complete the flower. Sew out the pairs into the small bars over the edge stitches. Tie and cut off the threads in the usual way. Work the tallies.
12. The leaves are worked next using five pairs of bobbins. At *f* sew two pairs into the centre pin, two pairs to the right into the edge of the braid, and one pair into the next pinloop.
13. Observe the worker line, working a four-about-the-pin edge in the centre of the leaf and a d st edge around the leaf. The first side may be worked in h st or broken spider, making one 'broken spider'. Observe the diagram (Fig 16). Work the second side in cl st.
14. Complete the leaves.

FIG 16 A broken spider, used to work the second side of the leaf, with a raised edge at the centre

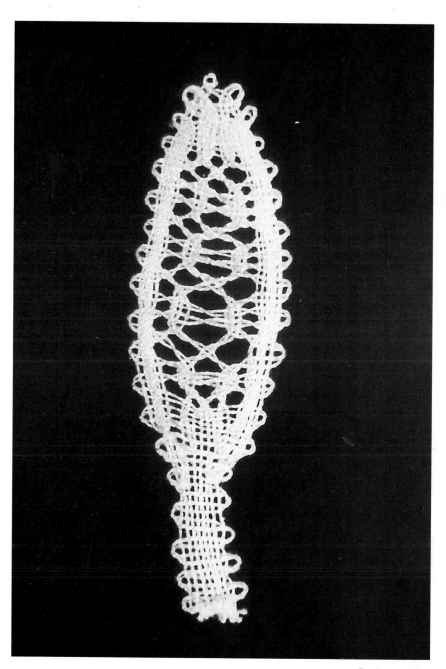

PHOTO 14 Broken spider

FIG 17 A pattern for the leaf in which the broken spider may be used

PHOTO 15 Flower no. 3 surrounded by edging no. 1

PHOTO 16 Flower no. 3 used in a paper weight

PHOTO 17 A doily 25cm in length

Chapter Three

Animals represented in lace

The representation of animals has always been popular in craftwork, and lacemaking has proved to be no exception. Four familiar animals have been chosen; one is used in a three-dimensional setting, using modern coloured threads, and two in a one-dimensional setting and the fourth, the butterfly, in either. The basic principles of Bruges Flower lace have been adhered to, and the techniques have been used to build up ideas for the animal designs. They are used in the form of pictures or domestic articles. They may be used on children's clothes, bags, aprons or tea-cosies.

MISS OWL Tanne thread no. 30

Techniques used in working the lace—leaves with h st vein, d st edge braid, false plait, sewings into a pinloop, filling no. 3.

Method of working the motif

1. Prepare the pricking as described on page 107.

The head
1. Start at *a* to work the crown. The two leaves are worked with a h st vein. After completing the second leaf, remember to tie the four remaining pairs down to the lace with a pair of bobbins which have been thrown out. (See *Bruges Flower Lace*, Chapter 7.)
2. At *b* sew in five pairs of bobbins. Use two pinloops and the edge of the braid between them. Complete the narrow d st edge braid. Sew out the threads using the two pinloops and the edge of the braid between the loops.
3. Start to work the d st edge braid for the eyes at *c*, using five pairs of bobbins. Work the false plait across each eye. When working the last eye, work the two plait-with-picots to join the two together.

4. Work the filling on each section.

The body
1. Work the lower leaves at *e*. They can be worked in either h st vein or ladder stitch. As the leaf narrows, throw out two pairs of bobbins and another two pairs at *f*. Six pairs remain to work the stem in d st edge braid, around the bottom of the owl and into the second leaf.
2. Work the last leaf, hanging in two pairs of bobbins in the next row, work two more rows and hang in another two pairs. Complete the leaf, throwing out eight pairs of bobbins as it narrows. Consult the photograph (Photo 18). Finish the tip of the leaf and after putting up the last pin, lay the two pairs between a pair of bobbins which has already been thrown out. Using this pair, tie them down to the lace. Cut off the threads.
3. Work the leaves near the head, by sewing into the lower leaves at *d*. They can be worked in either h st vein or ladder stitch. At the base of the leaf throw out four pairs. Six pairs remain to work the short d st edge braid. Sewings are made into the lower leaves.
4. Finish the braid by sewing out into the chin braid. Repeat at the other side of the owl.
5. Work the filling.

The branch
1. Along the line at *h* put up five pins. Hang two pairs of bobbins on each pin.
2. Work the branch using the d st edge braid. Marks are made on the branch with the use of 'ladder stitch', making twists with the worker pair.
3. Towards the division of the branch, hang in four more pairs of bobbins, 14 pairs of bobbins altogether.
4. Divide the branch with the addition of another pair. Use six pairs for the lower branch and nine

pairs for the upper branch. Complete the two
branches.

5. The threads should be tied off with one row of
knots only. The ends can be sewn through to the WS
with a needle. The beak, cut from leather, may be
stuck into position.

 Mount the owl on a background. Leaves can be
used to decorate the picture.

PHOTO 18 *Miss Owl*

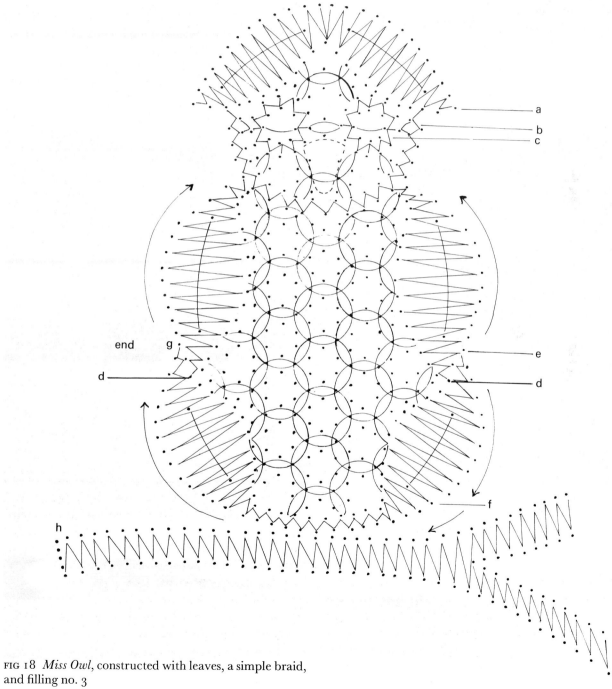

a
b
c
end g
d
e
d
f
h

FIG 18 *Miss Owl*, constructed with leaves, a simple braid, and filling no. 3

MASTER SEAHORSE Linen 100/2

The shape of the seahorse has been a challenge to
many craftswomen as a means of expressing the
techniques of her craft. Consequently this design was
evolved to use some of the basic techniques of Bruges
Flower lace.

Techniques used in working the motif—d st
edge braid, a tally, filling no. 1 Dieppe ground, d st
edge braid, plaits, plait-with-picots, sewing into a
pinloop, joining into a circle, b st, cl st.

Method of working the motif

1. Prepare the pricking as described on page 107.
2. Along a line at *a* put up three pins. Hang on five
pairs of bobbins.
3. Starting from the inner edge work a d st. Cl st
through two pairs, and work the d st edge.
4. Using this narrow d st edge braid work around the
head and across the top of the mouth. Note the b st
at the point. Take care to firm the threads.
5. Work the under section of the mouth. Sewings are
made into the pinloops of the top section.
6. Continue to work the braid. Observe the sewings
around the tail and especially the two sewings at the
end of the tail. Finish working the narrow braid and
when *a* is reached, join the braid together.
7. Work the braid of the fin by setting up at *b*, sewing
in three pairs to the braid. The braid widens quickly
so add two more pairs immediately. B st are used at
each corner. One row before completing the braid
throw out two pairs.
8. Sew out the three pairs at *c*. Tie and cut off the
threads.

The filling

Dieppe ground is used for this filling. Sew in the
pairs above the pin marks where they will be used.
Remember that the worker pair may be sewn out
and used as a passive pair. Sew out the pairs, do not
cut them off, and any alteration can be made to re-
align them. Then tie and cut off the threads. A tally
is used for the eye.

The edging

1. At *d* sew in four pairs of bobbins. These four pairs
are used to work the edging. Around the outer plait,
e, picots are made.
2. At *f* sew out all the pairs, tie and cut off the
threads.
3. At *g* sew in another four pairs of bobbins. Work

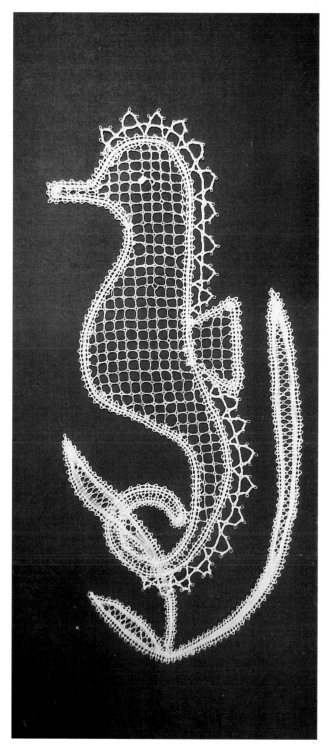

PHOTO 19 *Master Seahorse*, resting amongst the seaweed
fronds

the edging around the neck and head.
4. Sew out two pairs at *h* and after plaiting the
second two pairs, sew them out at *i*. Tie and cut off
the threads.

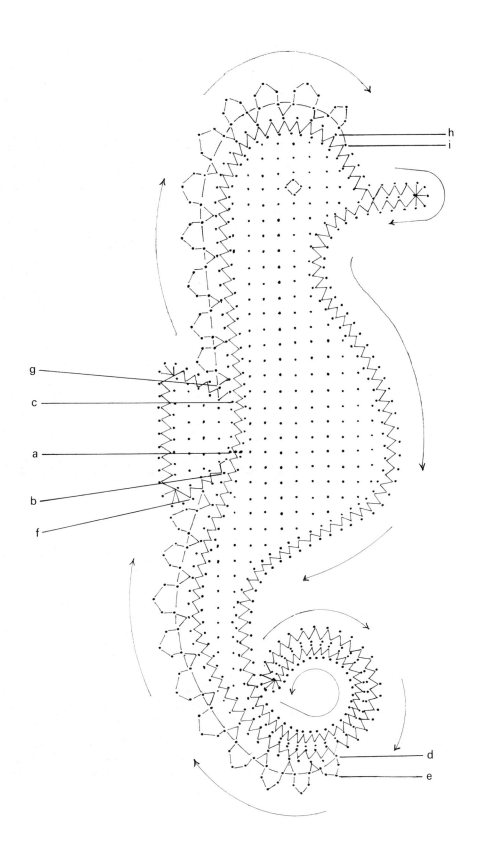

FIG 19 *Master Seahorse*, simple in shape, worked with a
simple braid, Dieppe ground, and half-stitch vein fronds

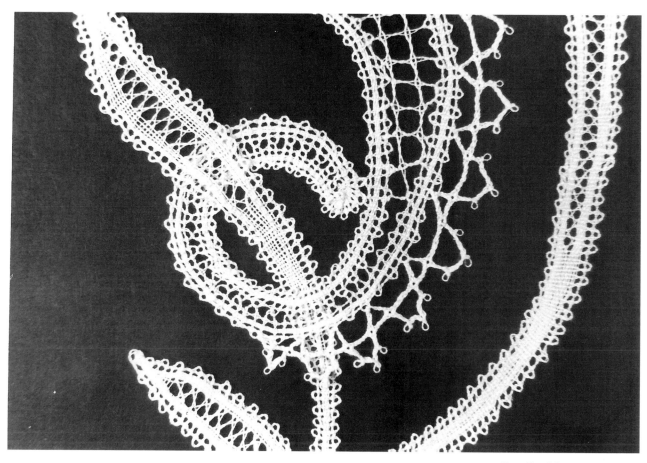

PHOTO 20 Details of the seahorse's tail

The seaweed

The fronds of the seaweed are labelled A, B and C. They are worked in that sequence. A and C are started as a single leaf.

Fronds A and B

1. Prepare the pricking as explained on page 107.
2. At *a* put up a pin. Hang two pairs of bobbins on the pin. Make two twists on the RH pair. Close the pin with a d st. These two pairs are used to work the edge stitch of the leaf.
3. At *b* put up a pin. Hang two pairs of bobbins on the pin. Make two twists on the RH pair. Using the RH pair from the centre pin work through both of these pairs in d st. Leave them.
4. At *c* put up a pin. Hang two pairs of bobbins on the pin. Make two twists on the RH pair. Work both of these pairs through the LH centre pair in d st. Allow both of these to hang as passive pairs. Leave them.
5. Examine diagram and using the RH pair from pin *b*, cl st through three pairs. Allow the worker pair to hang as a passive pair. At *d* put up a pin. Hang on two pair of bobbins as before. Make two twists on

the RH pair. Using the RH pair which has travelled from the centre pin at *a*, work a d st through both pairs.
6. Using the LH pair from *c*, cl st through four pairs. Leave them.
7. At *e* put up a pin. Hang on two pairs of bobbins. Make two twists on the RH pair. Using the LH pair from the centre pin at *a*, work a d st through both of these pairs. Leave them.
8. Using the RH pair from *d*, work through six pairs of bobbins in cl st. Allow the worker pair to hang as a passive pair, the LH pair from *e* now becomes the worker pair. Continue to work the leaf in cl st, keeping the d st edge. At *f* start to work the h st vein:
a. Work the d st edge. Cl st through three pairs, twist the workers and the next passive pair once.
b. Work one h st.
c. Cl st through three pairs and work the d st edge. Complete the frond using the h st vein until *g*. The frond continues to be worked in cl st only.
d. At *h* the frond narrows and one pair is thrown out. Select alternate threads. One pair is thrown out at *i* and *j*. These three pairs may be cut off later.

e. At *k* another pair is thrown out temporarily and brought back in again at *l*.

f. Between *l* and *m* hang in three more pairs. Ten pairs on the pillow.

g. At *m* start to work the h st vein, finishing at *n*.

h. At 'n' start to throw out two pairs on the next two rows.

i. Two pairs are left at the centre pin. Work the d st and take the pairs to the back of the pin. Open one of the thrown out pairs and place these two pairs between them and tie them down to the lace. Cut off the threads.

Frond C

1. Set up and work this frond as described in Frond A.

2. When *o* is reached start to work the h st vein finishing at *p*.

3. After working the pinhole at *q* throw out one pair. Reduce the pairs until five remain, sewing them out at the base of Frond B.

Mounting

On a pale blue background, place layers of blue and green tulle. Upon these layers place the seahorse and the fronds. The seahorse is attached to the fronds with his tail. Catch-stitch the motif to the background, between the pinloops.

FIG 20 The Fronds

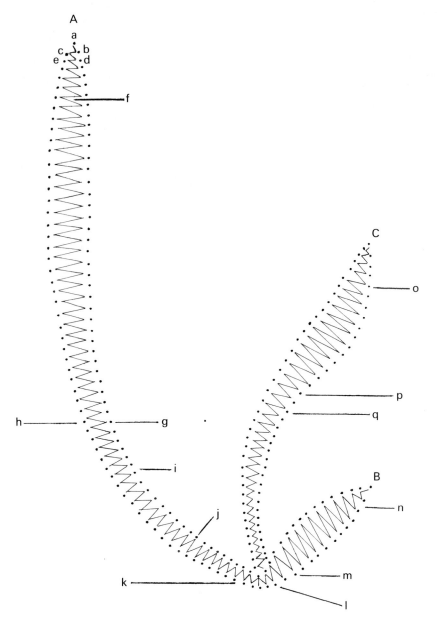

PHOTO 21 *Mrs Mouse*, a three-dimensional hold-all for lacemaking or needlework items, designed and worked by Mary Moseley

MRS MOUSE   DMC Retors d'Alsace no. 30

Mrs Mouse was designed as a three-dimensional project. It can be made from easily obtained household materials, i.e. a coffee jar, pieces of cotton fabric, ribbon, fur fabric, all of which may be found in the scrap box. She can be made by anyone with some needlework experience. Flowers, braids, and leaves are used to decorate the hat, pinafore, and dress, creating a novel holdall for lace or needlework equipment. You will see that no turnings are allowed on the patterns.

Materials

Pieces of fur fabric 48cm × 48cm; two plastic safety eyes; pipe cleaners; coffee jar with screw-top lid; glue; felt 30cm²; 1.5m × 1cm ribbon; 30cm × 3mm ribbon; 75mm PVC canvas circle; 5cm × 18.5cm PVC canvas; rayon raffia; kapok; pieces of fabric for the dress, pinafore and petticoat; no. 30 DMC Retors d'Alsace coloured threads; a ready-made straw hat.

Method of working the mouse

The tail
1. Fold the felt in half, stitch together and trim the seams. Examine the photograph for details (Photo 21).
2. Stuff the tail with pipe cleaners.

The body
Cut out the body section, with the fur pile running from top to bottom. Adjust the size to fit the jar. B st along the fitting line, trim down the turnings. Turn to the RS, and slide over the jar. Glue to the jar, turning under the raw edges.

The head
1. Cut out the head, and sew the eyes in place. Sew the seam. Using kapok, stuff the head firmly and when a good shape has been obtained glue the head over the edges of the lid.
2. The nose can be glued in position later.

The hands
1. Cut out in felt, stab stitch together.
2. Turn to the RS and stuff with kapok.

The arms
1. Make up the arms from the fur fabric, stuff carefully, and sew in position on the side of the lid. Attach the hands.
2. Sew a hook and eye to the wrist and fingers on the right hand to allow the mouse to hold the basket.

The ears
Using the felt, cut out and make up the ears. Attach the ears firmly to the hat as seen in the photograph (Photo 21).

The basket
The basket is made from the PVC plastic canvas and stitched with rayon raffia. It contains a tape measure and a pin cushion on top.

The pinafore
Cut out and make up the pinafore, allowing some fullness in the skirt. Attach the ribbons and the braid before the waistband is applied.

The petticoat
Make up the petticoat from white fabric. Put a gathering thread around the waist.

The dress
1. From the pieces of coloured cotton fabric cut out the dress. The dress must be 2 cm longer than the petticoat. Look at the instructions on the pattern of the bodice.
2. Use the press studs to fasten the back of the bodice.
3. The petticoat, and the dress skirt may be joined to the dress bodice at the same time.

Lace motifs
The following lace motifs are used to decorate Mrs Mouse: the hat, flower no. 2, page 47, Drieblad leaf, page 48; the pin cushion, flower no. 8, page 48; the dress, braid on a footing; the pinafore, braid with a hole, page 49, flower no. 3 on the bib, page 49, and flower no. 6 on the skirt, page 49. These are worked in coloured threads to match the printed cotton.

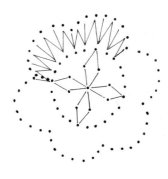

FIG 23 Flower no. 2, as used on the hat

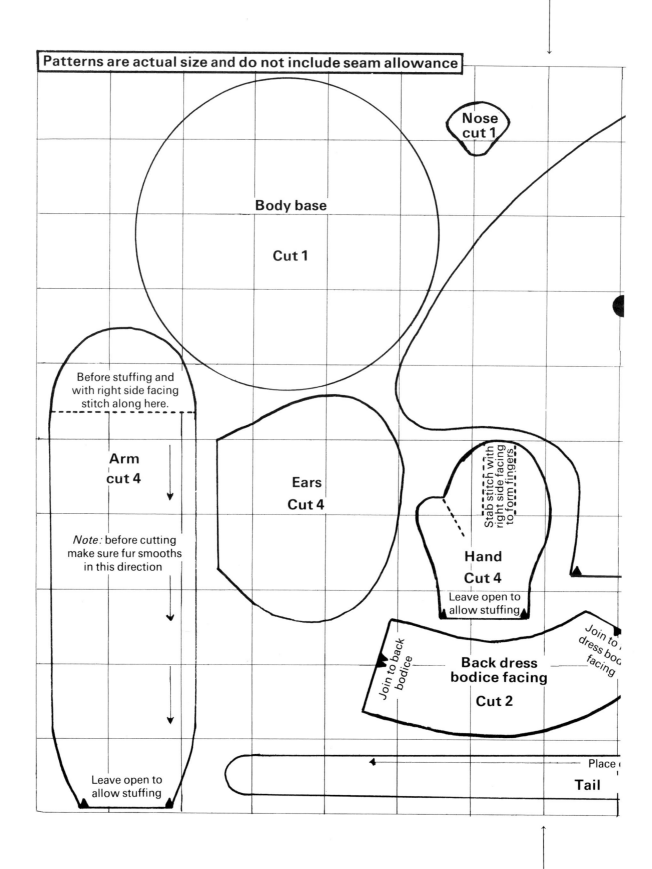

Patterns are actual size and do not include seam allowance

Nose
cut 1

Body base

Cut 1

Before stuffing and
with right side facing
stitch along here.

Arm
cut 4

Ears
Cut 4

Stab stitch with
right side facing
to form fingers

Hand
Cut 4

Note: before cutting
make sure fur smooths
in this direction

Leave open to
allow stuffing

Join to back
bodice

Back dress
bodice facing

Cut 2

Join to
dress bod
facing

Leave open to
allow stuffing

Place

Tail

FIG 21 Patterns are of actual size and do not include seam
allowances

44

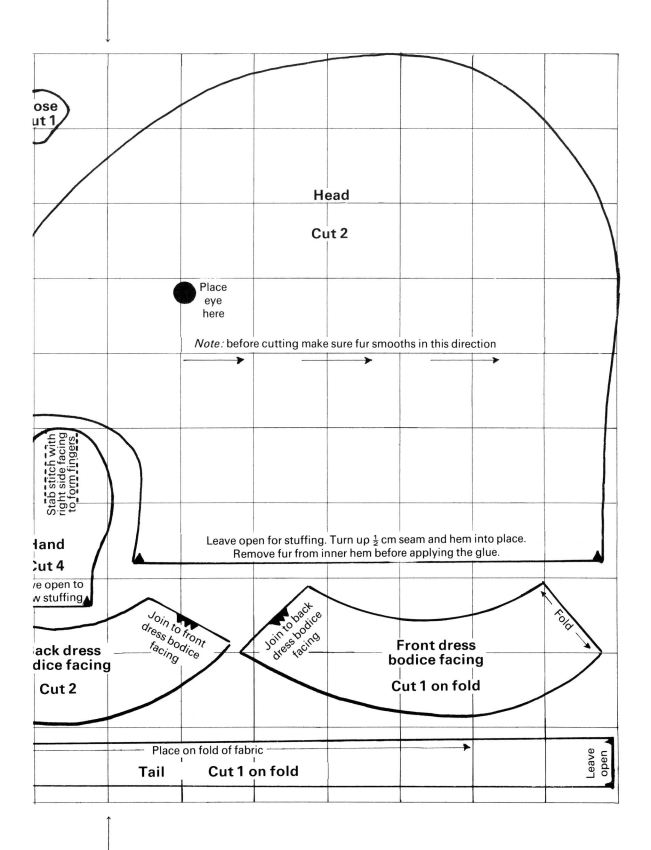

ose
ut 1

Head

Cut 2

Place
eye
here

Note: before cutting make sure fur smooths in this direction

Stab stitch with right side facing to form fingers

Hand

Cut 4

e open to
w stuffing

Leave open for stuffing. Turn up ½ cm seam and hem into place.
Remove fur from inner hem before applying the glue.

Join to front
dress bodice
facing

Join to back
dress bodice
facing

**ack dress
dice facing**

Cut 2

**Front dress
bodice facing**

Cut 1 on fold

Fold

Place on fold of fabric

Tail   **Cut 1 on fold**

Leave
open

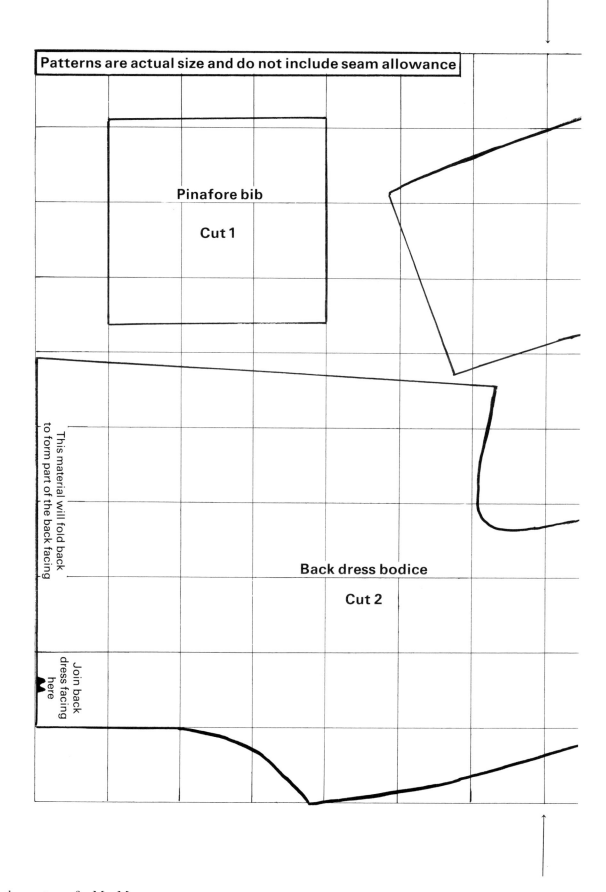

Patterns are actual size and do not include seam allowance

Pinafore bib

Cut 1

This material will fold back to form part of the back facing

Back dress bodice

Cut 2

Join back dress facing here

FIG 22 Further patterns for Mrs Mouse

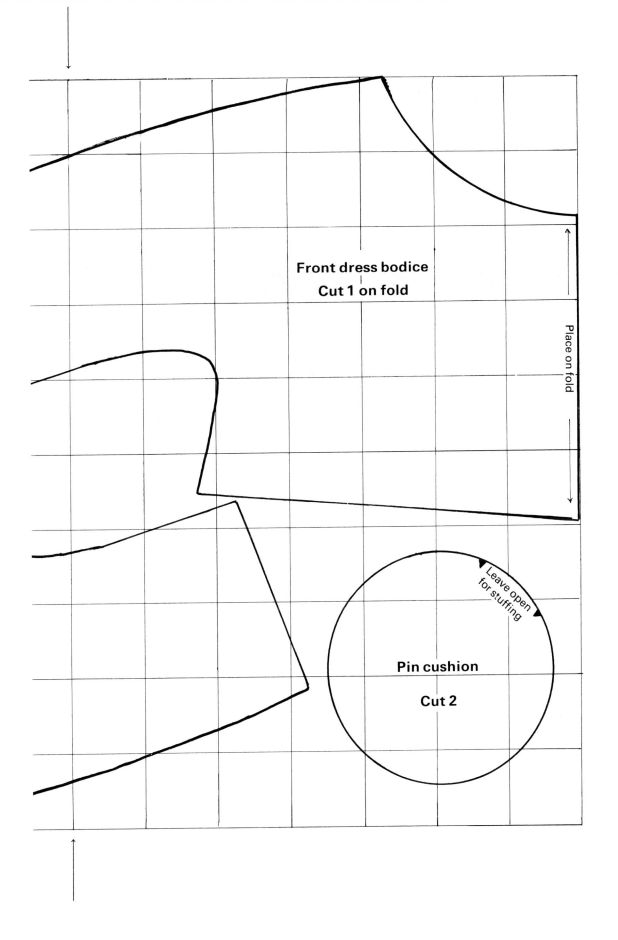

Front dress bodice

Cut 1 on fold

Place on fold

Leave open for stuffing

Pin cushion

Cut 2

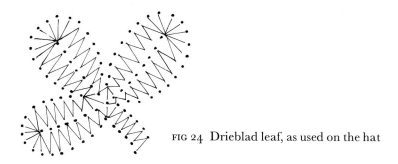

FIG 24 Drieblad leaf, as used on the hat

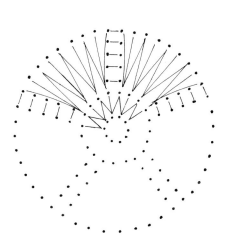

FIG 25 Flower no. 8, as used on the pincushion

FIG 26 Braid on a footing, as used on the dress

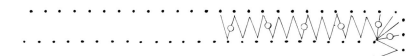

FIG 27 Braid with a hole, as used on the pinafore

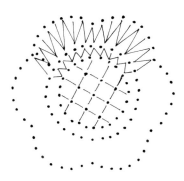

FIG 28 Flower no. 3, as used on the bib of the pinafore

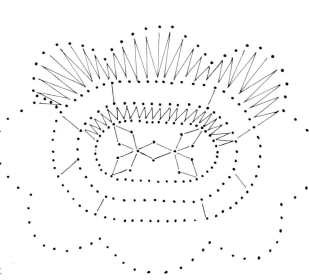

FIG 29 Flower no. 6, as used on the skirt

MR BUTTERFLY   Tanne thread no. 30

The butterfly makes a very pleasing picture. It can be mounted by sewing to a background fabric. The wings may be shaped by spraying with a weak solution of starch and laid over a curved surface to dry. This will give the impression of a butterfly in flight.

Techniques used in working the motif—Leaf with h st vein, plait, braid no. 1, scroll, filling no. 2, sewings, a ladder, h st, cl st, dividing a braid.

Method of working the motif

1. Prepare the pricking as described on page 107.
2. Start at the tip of the tail, *a*, by setting up exactly as described for the leaf with a h st vein, ten pairs of bobbins.
3. Work one row in cl st.
4. Hang in one pair at each side on the next row, and start to work the h st vein. Cease working the vein when *b* is reached.
5. Still using cl st work to the point marked *c*. Here, twist all the passive threads three times to make the waist.

PHOTO 22 *Mr Butterfly*, a motif full of detail and using many techniques

The thorax

1. Observe the photograph (Photo 22), and you will see that the thorax is decorated with a 'ladder', made by twists on the worker pair. Note that the centre pair is worked in cl st.

2. The thorax and the head are divided by working the 'ladder' at *d*, this time putting the twists on the passive pairs.

The head

1. The head is worked in h st. Throw out four pairs of bobbins as the size of the head decreases. Sixteen bobbins remain to work the antennae. The plait of each antenna is supported by placing a pin between the pairs.

2. Finish the plait by sewing into the pinloop. Tie off the threads and cut them close to the lace.

The wings

The braids which outline the wings are worked first. The scroll and the centre braid, enclosed within the outline braid, are worked next. The filling then links the two together.

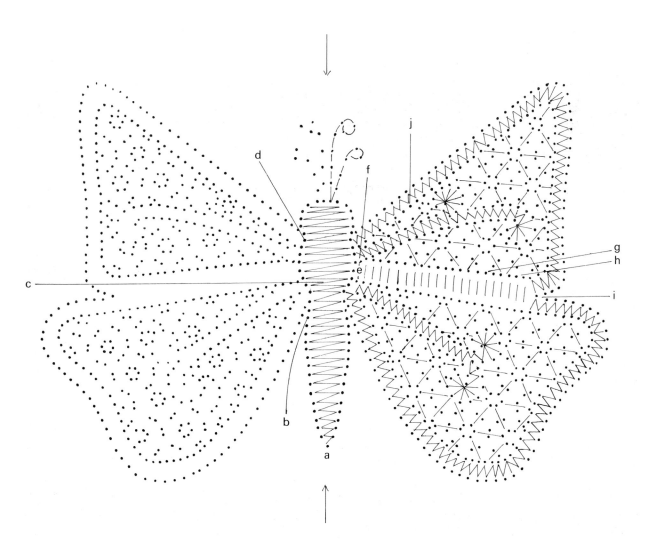

FIG 30 *Mr Butterfly*

The right wing

1. Sew in seven pairs of bobbins using the pinloops and the edge of the braid, at the point marked *e*.
2. Using the last pair on the left as workers, cl st through three pairs, twist the workers three times. Cl st through three pairs and put three twists on the worker pair.
3. Support this pair on a pin at *f* and work back across to the other edge making three twists on the worker pair in the centre.
4. Continue working the braid, and at *g* and *h*, hang in one pair of bobbins at each edge (11 pairs).
5. Reduce the twists to one at *i* and divide the braids.

The right upper wing

1. Using braid no. 1 and seven pairs of bobbins, work the outline braid for the front wing. Notice where the b st are worked at the tip of the wing. Sew out all the pairs into the thorax, using the pinloops and the edge of the braid. Tie and cut off the threads close to the lace.
2. Work the centre braid and the scroll by sewing five pairs of bobbins into the small area between the two braids.
3. As the division of the braid approaches, hang in two pairs of bobbins on each of the last two rows, four pairs of bobbins for each braid.
4. Divide the centre braid into two parts, using an extra pair to work this, as shown in chapter 6.
5. Finish the scrolls and lay aside two pairs of bobbins from the upper scroll to work the plait-with-picots in the narrow space at *j*. Sew out each pair into the braid.

6. Return to the main braid and work the second braid, using the new added pair as workers. Finish the braid and scroll. Before cutting off any pairs look and see if any can be used to work the filling of this wing.

The lower right wing

1. Using the four pairs already on the pillow, follow the worker line, and finish working the outline braid for the wing.
2. As the outline braid nears completion, it will be necessary to make sewings into the body of the butterfly.
3. Sew out the threads into the thorax. Lay two pairs of bobbins to one side to be used for the centre braid. Tie and cut off the threads.
4. Sew the two pairs for the centre braid into the pinloop between the outline and centre braids.
5. Hang in three more pairs of bobbins and work the centre braid as before. Two sewing are made into the lower outline braid and four sewings into the upper centre braid.
6. Divide the centre braid as before and work the scrolls.

The left wing

Follow the same pattern of work to complete the upper and lower wings.

The filling

Work filling no. 2, noting that it is worked from the outer edge of the wing toward the body. Pairs may be crossed over the scrolls and used lower down the wings.

Chapter Four

Mobiles

When travelling through the Low Countries my eyes are usually attracted to the houses and buildings fringing the road. It is very common to see elaborately decorated windows, using exotic plants, with a mobile as the centre attraction, often worked in hand-made lace. The shapes vary, being square, round, oval, or diamond. Sometimes the shape resembles a large curved fire screen. Five mobiles have been designed with alternative uses, such as a picture or a doily.

REGULUS   Linen 60/2

This motif may be used as a mobile, mounted into a 12cm frame, or by adding a simple edging it is ideal for use as a coaster. The flower is known as the Chinese Rose.

Techniques used in working the motif—cl st, h st, false plait, plaits, flower no. 9, d st edge braid, joining into a circle, b st, sewings.

Method of working the motif

Inner circle
1. Prepare the pricking as described on page 107.
2. Along the line at *a* put up four pins. Hang on seven pairs of bobbins, side by side.
3. Using the first pair on the inner edge as workers, cl st to the outer edge. Work the d st edge. Return to the inner edge in cl st and work the d st edge. Firm the passive threads.
4. Work the inner circle in this manner, noting where the b st are worked, until *b* is reached.
5. The filling is worked before completing the inner circle. Work the edge stitch at *b* and using the LH

pair of the edge pairs, twist them three times. Put up a pin at *c*, hang on one pair of bobbins. Using these two pairs work a cl st, pin, cl st (at *c*). Work in an anti-clockwise direction.
6. Plait to *d*, put up a pin in the centre of the two pairs. Work the false plait to *e* and back to *d*. Finish the filling, using plaits and false plaits until *c* is reached. Sew into *c*. Throw out one pair of bobbins at *c*. Tie them off carefully and lay them to the back of the work. Cut them off upon completion of the inner circle.
7. From the back of the twisted pair and using a crochet hook, ease through one of the threads and slide the other thread through the loop. Ease the threads towards the inner circle. Make a sewing at *b*, work a d st and finish working the inner circle.
8. Join the circle in the usual way. Tie off all the threads and cut them close to the lace.

The petals
1. Along the line at *f* put up five pins and hang two pairs of bobbins on each pin. From *g* work a row of h st to the outer edge. Work the d st edge and return to the inner edge, which is worked as a d st edge.
2. Work the flower completely in h st, noting where the b st and the false plaits are worked.
3. Join the threads to the starter pinloops, one pair of threads to one pinloop. Tie off all the threads and cut them off close to the lace.

The frame braid
1. Along the line at *h*, put up three pins. Hang on five pairs of bobbins, side by side.
2. Work the narrow braid in cl st with a d st edge at both inner and outer edges. Sewings are made into the points of the petals.

3. Join the threads in the usual way, tying and cutting them off close to the lace.

For a coaster work the plait-with-picot edging.

Mounting

The frame used for this mobile was already enamelled and does not require any further treatment. If the frame is untreated it should be painted with white enamel paint. The motif should be overcast through each pinloop to attach it to the frame, using a fine Coton Perle thread.

PHOTO 23 *Regulus*, ideal for use as a mobile or coaster

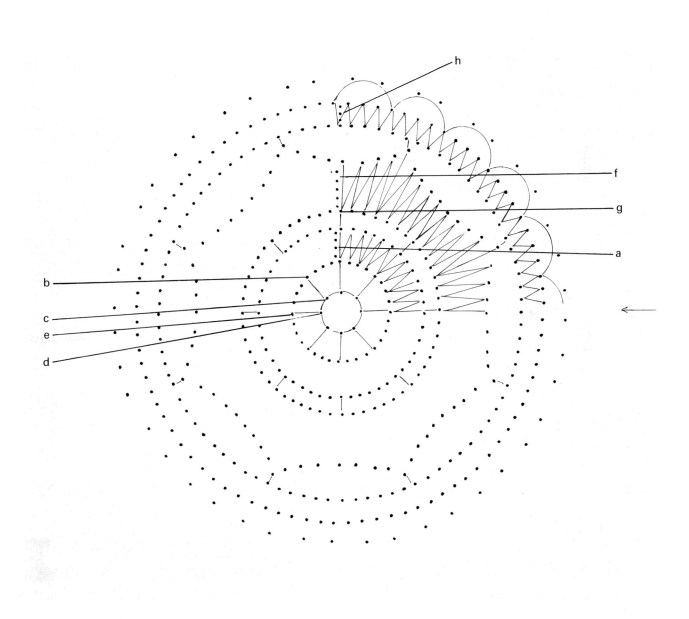

FIG 31 *Regulus*, a mobile or doily, worked in 60/2 linen
thread

PYXIS   Linen 60/2

Pyxis is comprised of many basic techniques, and may be worked as a mobile or as a doily. Christmas ribbons, red and green, can be attached to the lower edge of the mobile and suspended over the dining table during the festive period. Another method of working the lily will be used.

Techniques used in working the motif—cl st, h st, d st, d st edge braid, sewings, raised edge sewings, a scroll, filling no. 3, a lily, plait, plait-with-picot, edging no. 3.

PHOTO 24 *Pyxis* introduces another method of working a lily

FIG 32 *Pyxis*, a mobile, introducing the lily worked in
another method

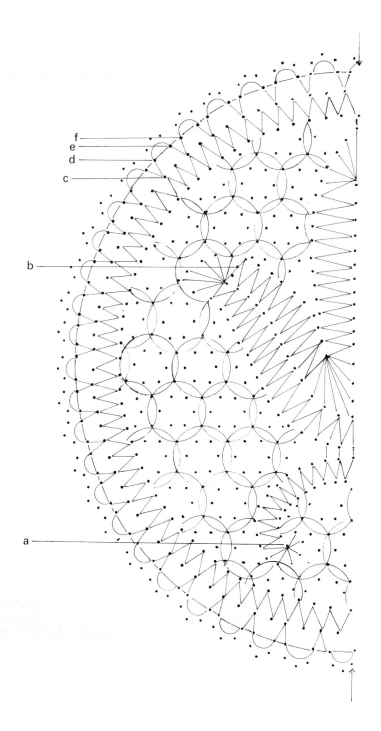

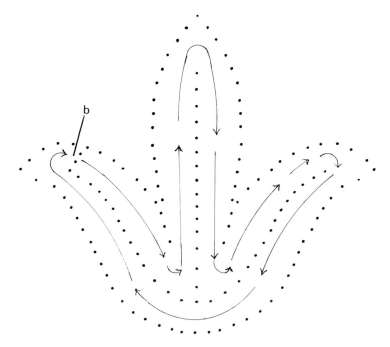

FIG 33 Arrows indicate the direction in which the lily is worked

Method of working the motif

1. Make the whole pattern and prepare the pricking as described on page 107.

2. Start by working the scroll at *a* (chapter 6), using five pairs of bobbins. Work the short braid and finish the scroll.

3. Look at the pricking and you will see that the lily is set up at *b*. Along the line at *b* on the LH petal, put up four pins and hang on nine pairs of bobbins, side by side.

4. Using h st, follow the worker line, using 'four-about-the-pin' (straight edge) at the centre of the LH petal and a d st edge at the outer edge.

5. At the base of the LH petal, b st are used to pivot the braid round to work the centre petal. False plaits are worked at the base of the lily. At the halfway (pivot) point change to cl st. Remember to make a sewing through all the threads about the pivot pin (using the extra thread as described in chapter 6).

6. Complete the first side of the centre petal, taking the cl st round the top of the leaf. Make a sewing through the loops about the centre pin. The second side is worked in h st sewing into the bars, to make the raised edge. Refer to the photograph (Photo 24).

7. Work the RH petal, following the worker line, making the sewings under both the bars down the centre for the raised edge. Note where the stitch changes to cl st. Sewings are made into the bars, resulting in a raised edge.

8. Finish the RH petal, taking the cl st around the top of the petal. Work the last section of the LH petal. Join the threads at *b*, sewing one pair into one pinloop. Do not disfigure the edge pinloop.

The frame braid
Follow the instructions for the braid in Pyxis.

The filling
Filling no. 3 has been used for this motif.

Mounting

1. Apply two coats of paint to a 14cm round frame.
2. Using DMC Cotton Perle no. 5, blanket stitch around the frame.
3. With a coloured thread mark four equal sections of the frame and the motif. Place the coloured threads together and catch stitch them in place.
4. Sew them together, by making a stitch into each pinloop and the blanket stitched edge.
5. Remove the coloured threads.

The edging, for a doily

1. At *c* sew in two pairs of bobbins. Plait to *d*. Join in two more pairs of bobbins.
2. With the RH set of bobbins work the plait-with-picots. The LH set will work the plait to *e*, where they are joined with a windmill.
3. Take up the LH set and work the plait towards the braid. A sewing is made into the braid. Firm the threads and plait to *f*.
4. The RH set of bobbins will plait to *f*. The two sets of bobbins are joined with a windmill.
5. Complete the edging, carefully sewing out both sets of bobbins.

ORION Linen 60/2

This motif was designed as a revision exercise of basic techniques, worked in circles for use as a mobile. Do not be discouraged from working the motif by the presence of the leaf plaits. They are a challenge and the task will be rewarding. When working the braids and the leaf plaits, make sure that the bobbins are fully wound.

There are two methods of working this motif.

Techniques used in working the motif—flower no. 5, d st edge braid, h st, cl st, sewings, false plait, a leaf plait, four-about-the-pin edge (straight edge), hole in the braid, joining into a circle, tying off several threads.

First method of working the motif

1. Make the whole pattern as described in chapter 1.
2. Prepare the pricking as described on page 107.
3. Work flower no. 5 as described on page 69, in *Bruges Flower Lace*. Set up the inner circle at *a*, and the petals along the line at *b*.

Braid A
All the setting up lines of the braids must be in a straight line, radiating from the centre point. Make sure the bobbins are fully wound.
1. Along the line at *c*, put up seven pins. Hang on two pairs of bobbins on each pin, side by side.

PHOTO 25 *Orion*

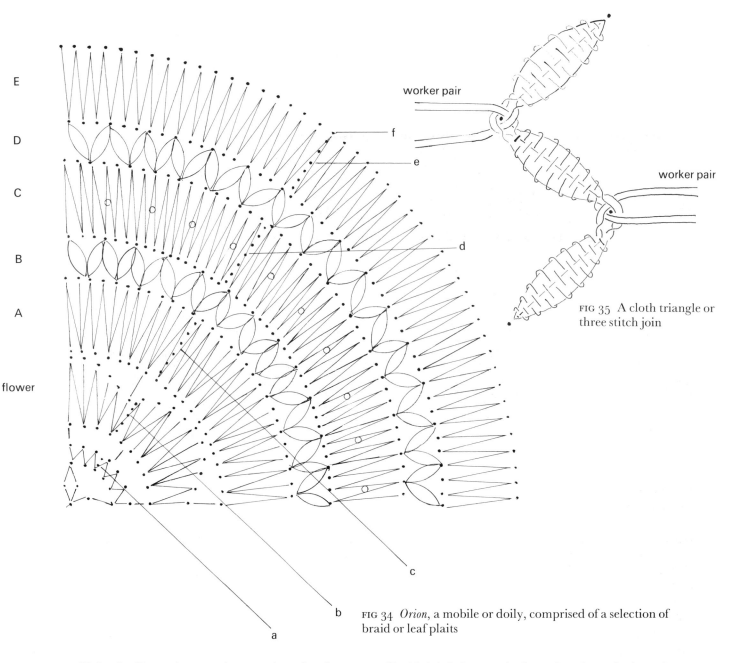

E

D

C

B

A

flower

f

e

d

c

b

a

worker pair

worker pair

FIG 35 A cloth triangle or three stitch join

FIG 34 *Orion*, a mobile or doily, comprised of a selection of braid or leaf plaits

2. Take the first pair as workers, and work a d st edge. Using h st work to the outer edge where a d st edge is worked.

3. Follow the worker line back to the inner edge and work the d st edge. Continue in this way, noting where the sewings are made into the pinloops of the petals. A false plait is worked to join the braid to the petal.

4. Complete the braid and join it into a circle, sewing one pair into one pinloop. Take care not to lose the twist on each pair. Tie off the threads in the usual way. Cut off the threads close to the lace.

Braid B

The leaf plaits may be worked at the same time as

Braid A is being worked, sewing the pairs into the pinloops of the braid.

1. Start by sewing in two pairs into the pinloop, and work the leaf plait. Put up a pin between the two pairs—a twist on each pair—turn the pillow and work a leaf plait back towards the braid.

2. The leaf plaits must not be made too long. Sew into the pinloop. Finish all the leaf plaits, sew out and tie off the threads.

Braid C

1. Along a line at *d* put up seven pins. Hang on 14 pairs of bobbins, side by side.

2. Start the braid as before, but this time using cl st. The 'hole' is worked at every fourth pin, counting on

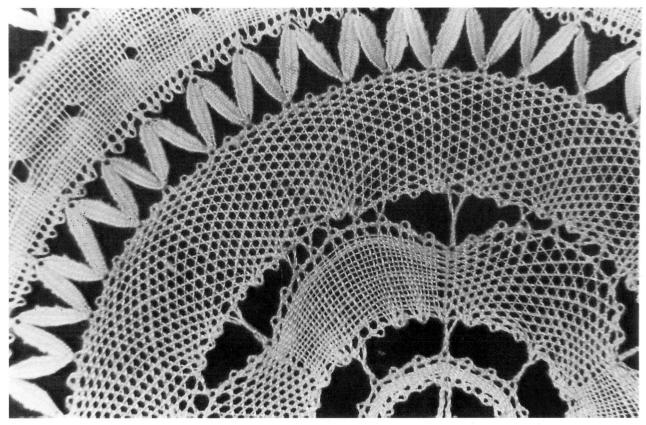

PHOTO 26 A section of *Orion* illustrating a braid with a hole and leaf plaits

the inner edge.

3. Cl st through five pairs of bobbins. Leave the workers as passive threads. Take up the next pair of passive threads to use as workers.

4. Cl st through five pairs of bobbins. Work the d st edge. Care must be taken not to pull the old or new worker threads. Keep the hole small by negotiating the passive threads towards the centre of the braid.

5. Work back to the inner edge, work the d st edge, and complete the braid in this way, remembering to sew into the pinloop of the leaf plaits.

6. When *d* is reached, join the braid into a circle, one pair being sewn into one pinloop about the starter pin.

Braid D

The leaf plaits may be worked together with Braid C, sewing into a pinloop of Braid C, as before.

Braid E

1. Along a line at *e* put up seven pins. Hang on two pairs on each pin, side by side.

2. With the two pairs at *f*, work a d st, with an extra twist on each pair.

3. Using h st work towards the inner edge. Work the d st edge.

4. Return to the outer edge, using h st and work a four-about-the-pin edge (straight edge). Look at the photograph (Photo 26). Continue to work the braid. Make the sewings into the small hole between the leaf plaits.

5. Join the braid into a circle as before, taking care not to lose the twist on each pair. Carefully tie off the threads. Cut off the threads close to the lace.

Second method of working the motif

1. Work all the braids with all the pairs at the same time. Make a link with the leaf plaits and the worker pair of the braid, using a cloth triangle or three-stitch join—cross, twist, cross—with the pairs. Note that the workers will change.

Mounting

The 26cm frame used for this mobile was already enamelled and does not require any further treatment. If the frame is untreated it should be painted with white enamel paint. The motif should be overcast through each pinloop to attach it to the frame, using a fine Coton Perle thread.

PHOTO 27 *Cygnus 1*

THE SWANS

Those of you who have visited the old part of Bruges, may remember the swans, geese and ducks wandering about the shores of the lake. The swans have proved to be very popular features of Bruges Flower lace and they are to be seen on many domestic pieces of lace; their shape offers great scope for the designer. Cygnus 1 and Cygnus 2 have been designed to show the effect of simplicity, allowing the braids and stitches to make the design.

CYGNUS 1   Tanne thread no. 30

Techniques used in working the motif—Braid no. 1, dividing a braid, sewings, a ladder, h st vein, hanging in a pair, throwing out a pair in cl st and h st, cl st, h st, plait, b st false plait.

Method of working the motif

1. Prepare the pricking as described on page 107.
2. At *a* put up a pin. Hang on three pairs of bobbins.

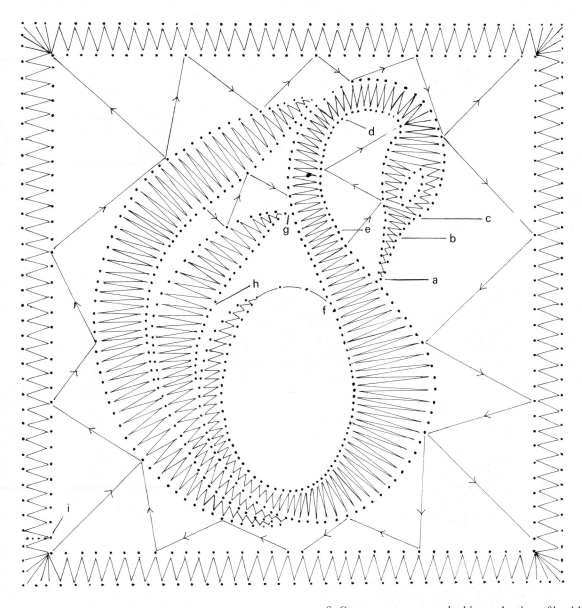

FIG 36 *Cygnus 1*, a swan, worked in a selection of braids

3. Start to work the beak by using the LH pair of bobbins as workers. Cl st through two pairs, twist the workers twice and support them on a pin. Work across the two pairs, twist the workers twice and support them on a pin.

4. As the beak widens hang in two more pairs at *b*, and when *c* has been worked there should be seven pairs of bobbins.

5. Divide the braid, three pairs at each side, and work the braid over the eye first. Leave them. Using the second worker, added when the braid was divided (chapter 6), work the lower braid. Join the two worker pairs together at the centre pin. Continue to work the head, hanging in four more pairs, one pair in each row at the outer edge. Leave the RH pair as passive threads and use the LH pair as workers. With this pair work out to the LH edge of the braid. Continue working the neck.

6. It may be necessary to throw out a pair of bobbins in each row at the RH edge of the braid. The neck is still becoming slimmer and by the time *d* is worked ten pairs should remain.

PHOTO 28 Three braids used in the working of *Cygnus 1*

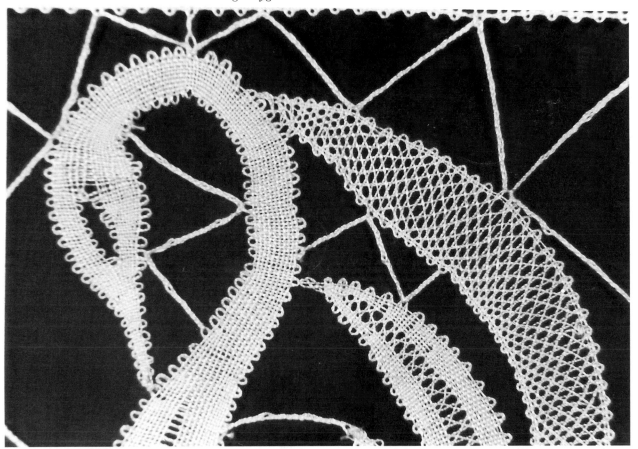

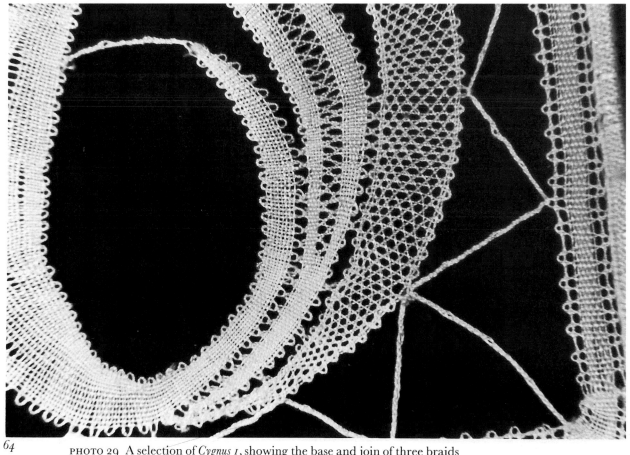

PHOTO 29 A selection of *Cygnus 1*, showing the base and join of three braids

7. Continue to work the neck. At *e* the neck widens and six more pairs are added at intervals down the RH edge, making 16 pairs in all. Work a sewing at *a* to join the body and the beak together.

8. As the pairs are added to accommodate the width of the body, a ladder stitch may be introduced as you can see in the photograph.

9. As the body narrows, the ladder stitch will not be needed. Throw out pairs at the LH edge until five pairs remain. Finish the tail feather but when working the last three rows throw out one pair on each row. With the two remaining pairs work a plait, and support the plait with a pin between the pairs at the two pin marks. Sew out each pair into the body of the swan at *f*.

10. Start to work the centre feather by sewing two pairs of bobbins into the loop of the neck at *g*. Hang in two more pairs of bobbins.

11. Using braid no. 1, work four rows in cl st, putting two twists on the worker pair, supporting them on a pin. Start to work the h st vein. Hang in two more pairs of bobbins in each row, until 12 pairs are on the pillow. Work the braid until *h* is reached.

12. Here throw out one pair of bobbins at the RH edge.

13. Sewings are used to join this feather to the first one. At the same time throw out two pairs on each row—one pair at each edge on the same row. Two and a half centimetres from the end of this feather stop working the h st vein.

14. Continue in cl st, using six pairs of bobbins. Towards the last few pins throw out three more pairs of bobbins and sew out the remaining three pairs into the base of the swan. Tie and cut off the threads.

15. Work the last feather in h st setting up as for a leaf, keeping a pair of passive threads at each side to be worked in cl st. Add more pairs, until six pairs are in use.

16. Continue to work the feather, making sewings into every fourth loop of the centre feather. Reduce the passive threads as the feather narrows. Throw out the pairs at the RH edge. Five pairs remain.

17. Work the last 12 rows (six pins each side) in cl st. Make sewings into the centre feather using the last four RH loops of the feather. Throw out two pairs of bobbins and sew out the three remaining pairs into the base of the swan. Tie and cut off the threads.

The frame braid

1. At *i* put up five pins. Hang on seven pairs of bobbins. Using a d st edge braid, work the braid in a clock-wise direction.

2. Note the b st at the corner of the braid, and the false plait worked at the base of the swan.

3. Finally join the braid in the usual way. Tie the threads and cut them off close to the lace.

The filling

The plaits are worked in a direction shown by small arrows. They are supported along the line by putting up a pin between the pairs. Work the next section of the plait. Sew into the appropriate pinloop of the braid or swan. Remove the pins and press the motif between damp linen fabric.

Mounting

1. Apply two coats of paint to a 15cm frame.

2. Using a spool of DMC Coton Perle no. 5, blanket stitch around the frame.

3. With a coloured thread mark the centre of each side of the frame and the motif. Place the coloured threads together and catch stitch them in place.

4. Sew them together, by making a stitch into each pinloop and the blanket stitched edge.

5. Remove the coloured threads.

CYGNUS 2   Tanne thread no. 30

This swan has been designed specially to use a simple braid, mounted as a mobile or a picture. The space between the braids accommodates filling no. 3, a plait-with-picot, which is worked when the swan is completed. A 15cm metal frame is required for mounting the swan.

Techniques used in working the motif—cl st, sewings, dividing a braid, filling no. 3, plaits, h st vein, b st, hanging in a pair, throwing out a pair, joining a braid.

Method of working the motif

1. Prepare the pricking as described on page 107.

2. Start at the point of the beak, by putting up a pin at *a*. Hang on four pairs of bobbins.

3. Take up the RH pair as workers, work across the three pairs to the left in d st. Put an extra twist on the workers. Put up a pin under the worker pair at the edge. Return to the opposite edge. Finish working the beak.

4. At *b* change to cl st. Hang in one more pair of bobbins at the beginning of the next four rows, still keeping the simple edge.

5. At *c* divide the braid equally (refer to chapter 6), ready for working two braids around the eye. Work the two braids, joining them at *d*. Allow one pair of workers to hang as a passive pair. Hang in one more

PHOTO 30 *Cygnus 2*

pair at the neck edge, ten pairs should be on the pillow.

6. Work the neck, b st at the inner edge of the curve. Throw out three pairs, one pair in each row, as the neck narrows.

7. Seven pairs remain to work the braid. At *e* start to work the h st vein. Finish working the h st vein at *f*, and continue the braid in cl st. Refer to the technical drawing and the photograph and note where the sewing, false plaits, and b st are worked (Fig 37 and Photo 30).

8. Gradually taper the braid by throwing out pairs until three pairs remain. Sew them out into the braid. Tie and cut off the threads close to the lace.

9. Work the areas of plait-with-picot filling.

The frame braid
This braid is worked as for Cygnus 1.

The plait filling
This filling is worked as in Cygnus 1.

Mounting

Follow the instructions for Cygnus 1.

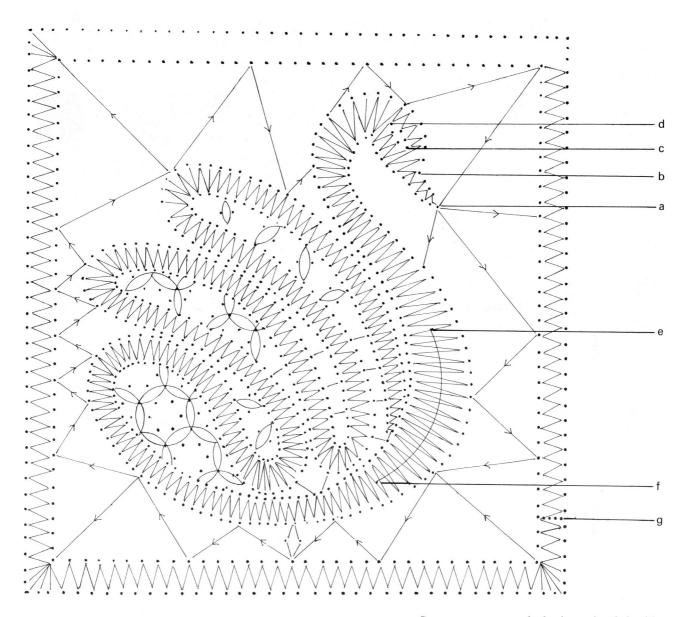

FIG 37 *Cygnus 2*, a swan, worked using a simple braid

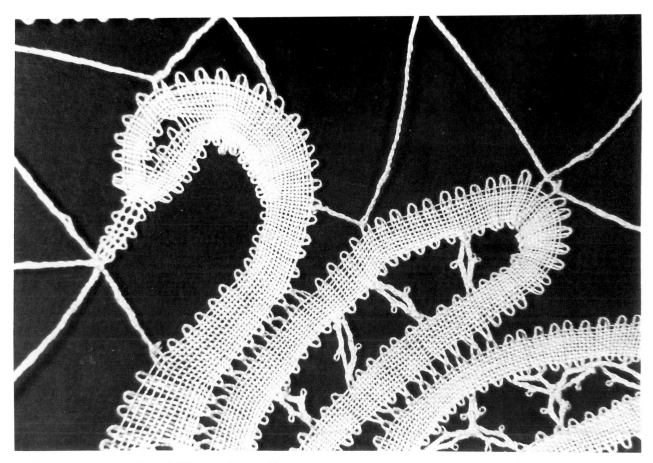

PHOTO 31 A simple braid and filling used in working
Cygnus 2

C h a p t e r   F i v e _____

More projects

In this chapter, the basic techniques have been brought together to produce several designs. These designs entail the use of these techniques to an advanced level. Experience in working Bruges Flower lace will solve many of the problems of setting up, judging when to hang in and throw out pairs in this artistic lace. Good tension is essential for a neat appearance of the lace. All the threads should be firmed at the end of each row. Make sure the bobbins are fully wound, that the pins are placed into the card in the right direction, and the threads are all the same length. Consult chapter 6 frequently to ensure adherence to the methods used in *Bruges Flower Lace*. Mounting the lace will be described when all the pieces of lace are finished.

PHOTO 32 *Cetus Major*

DINNER MATS, PANELS

CETUS MAJOR   Linen 60/2

This motif was designed to include flower no. 6, braids, scrolls and a new filling. This filling is worked in two ways. The first one is used in the main design and the variation of the filling, in the small motif.

Techniques used in working the motif—flower no. 6, cl st, h st, d st edge braid, false plaits, plait-with-picot, filling no. 7, sewings, sewing into a braid, a windmill, a scroll.

Method of working the motif

The outer braid
1. Make the whole pattern. Prepare the pricking as described on page 107.
2. Along a line at *a* put up four pins. Hang two pairs of bobbins on each pin, side by side.
3. Using cl st work a d st edge braid.
4. Look at the technical drawing and you will see

that the top and the bottom corners are worked in a different manner.
5. Join the braid carefully, tie and cut off the threads close to the lace.

Centre of the motif
1. At *b* start to work the scroll, using the same braid as before. Hang in pairs until there are eight pairs of bobbins on the pillow.
2. By consulting the photograph you will be able to see where sewings have been made into the outer braid at various points *c*. B st are used to work around the curve of this braid.
3. Complete the braid remembering to work more sewings to join the scroll to the braid.
4. Finish the braid by working the second scroll, noting the b st and the sewings.
5. A further examination of the photograph (Photo 33) will show that the flower is set up by sewing six pairs

PHOTO 33 Details of *Cetus Major*

of bobbins into the pinloops and the edge of the braid, to work the inner circle. The filling cannot be worked in the usual way. When the inner circle is completed, sew two pairs of bobbins into the braid and use these to work the filling.

6. Work the petals next, by sewing ten pairs of bobbins into the pinloops and the edge of the braid.

7. Complete the petals, remembering to work the false plaits, joining the inner circle and the petals together. Note that one false plait is worked to join the petal to the outer braid.

The honeycomb filling

1. Sew in pairs above the marked pinholes. Use single pairs to work the filling.

2. Where the threads join at a pinhole, make three or four twists on each pair, h st pin, h st, make three or four twists on each pair.

3. Where the threads join (without a pinhole), a cl st only is used, make three or four twists on each pair. Work the small areas, e.g. *d*.

FIG 38 *Cetus Major*, the first dinner mat

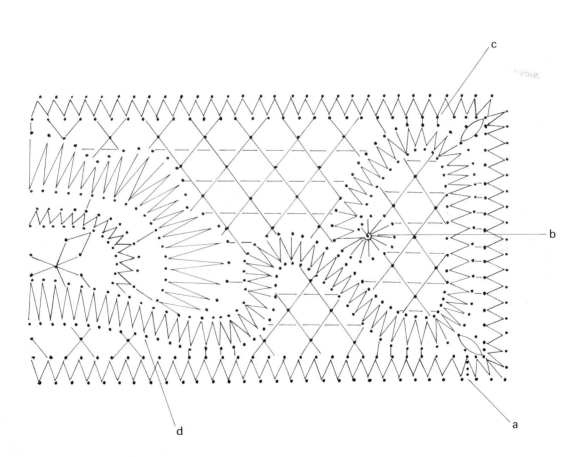

CETUS MINOR

1. Start with the scroll at *a*, and work the short braid, using eight pairs of bobbins. Note the two false plaits used to join the two braids together. Finish the motif by working the scroll at *b*.
2. Look at the technical drawing and sew in pairs above the marked pinholes. The honeycomb filling is worked by using a closed pin whenever two pairs of bobbins are joined together. Put three or four twists on each pair to start with, h st, pin, h st, make two or three twists on each pair.

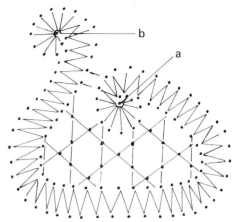

FIG 39 *Cetus Minor*, the small corner motif

PHOTO 34 *Cetus Minor*

PERSEUS MAJOR   Linen 60/2

The second dinner mat has been designed to include another simple braid and filling.

Techniques used in working the motif—d st edge braid, cl st, h st, d st, plait-with-picot, Dieppe ground, sewings, false plait, b st.

Method of working the motif

The outer braid
1. Make the complete pattern and prepare the pricking as described on page 107.
2. Work the Outer Braid as described in Cetus.

Centre of the motif
1. Look at the photograph of this motif (Photo 35). Start by working the scroll at the LH side of the motif, increasing the number of pairs until there are six pairs of bobbins on the pillow.
2. Using cl st work the d st edge braid. Note where the b st are worked and the sewings are made into the outer braid.
3. Finish the braid and work the scroll at the RH side of the motif.
4. Work the three 'leaf shapes' next. Sew in six pairs of bobbins equally into the pinloops and the edge of the braid at *a*.
5. Follow the worker line carefully and using cl st work the RH side. Hang in two more pairs of bobbins.
6. When the pinhole at *b* has been worked, work a row of d st towards the inner edge. The middle section is worked in h st. Note the sewings which are made into the outer braid.
7. At *c* work a row of d st, and work the last section in cl st, working the plait-with-picot filling where marked. As the section narrows, throw out two pairs of bobbins. Finish this side. Sew out the pairs into the pinloops and the edge of the braid. Work the other two 'leaf shapes'.

The filling
Dieppe ground has been used in this motif. Sew in the pairs where needed, work the area. Sew them into the edge of the braid etc., and leave them. By taking the threads over the braids they may be used again. If so, tie them once after the sewing, twist the pair, and sew them in again where needed. Use each pair for as long as possible, without tying, cutting off and resewing into a pinloop.

PHOTO 35 *Perseus Major*

PHOTO 36 Details of *Perseus Major*

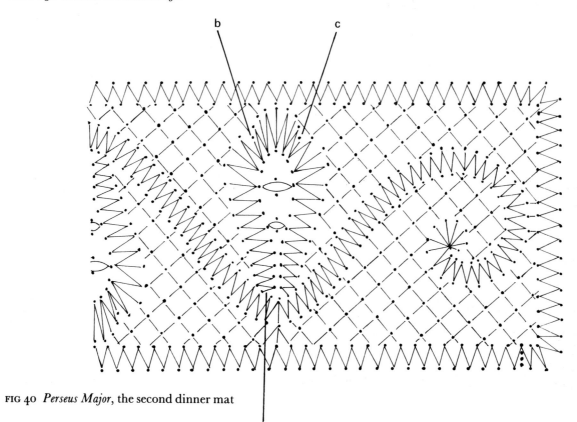

FIG 40 *Perseus Major*, the second dinner mat

74

PERSEUS MINOR

This motif is set up at *a*. Complete the first scroll.
Work the short braid in cl st, using six pairs of
bobbins, and finishing with the second scroll at *b*.
Work the leaf shape as previously described.

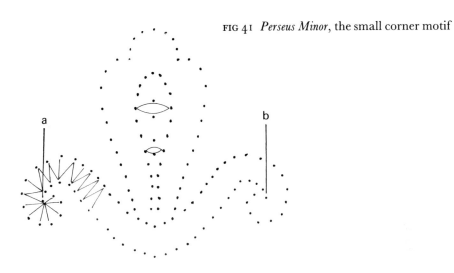

FIG 41 *Perseus Minor*, the small corner motif

PHOTO 37 *Perseus Minor*

TAURUS MAJOR Linen 60/2

In this design another method of working leaves has been introduced. They are worked in two sections. The lower leaves are worked first and then the centre leaf. The leaves are worked in h st and cl st, so as to resemble an individual leaf. Care should be taken to ensure that the correct number of bobbins remain to work the appropriate stitch as bobbins are thrown out. Tie the pairs in a reef knot when thrown out in h st.

Techniques used in working the motif—cl st, h st, d st, sewings into a raised edge, raised edge (straight edge), flower no. 7, d st edge braid, tally, filling no. 2.

Method of working the motif

1. Make the complete pattern and prepare the pricking as described on page 107.
2. Work the outer braid as described in Cetus.

Centre of the motif

1. Work the centre flower first. The inner circle requires six pairs of bobbins worked with a raised edge and the petals require eight pairs of bobbins. Follow the worker lines carefully, consulting the photograph frequently.
2. Take care to firm the threads. Shape the passive threads to follow the outer curve and keep the small plaits short.
3. The half flowers are worked next. Set up by using the pinloops and the edge of the braid between the loops for the sewings. Work it in a similar way as working a complete flower. (*Bruges Flower Lace,* flower no. 7.)
4. Work the leaves by putting up four pins along the line at *a*. Hang on six pairs of bobbins. Twist each pair once.
5. Using the two pairs on the RH pin, work a d st. Using h st work towards the inner edge. A raised edge is worked down the centre of each leaf.
6. Follow the worker line carefully. Note the b st and where the stitch changes to cl st at the base of the leaf.
7. Hang in two pairs to work the cl st area. When working the tip of the leaf throw out three pairs at the inner edge. Five pairs will work the h st area.
8. Finish working the leaves in this manner. At the base of the leaves note that two false plaits and three sewings are worked into the outer braid. The stitch changes to cl st at the halfway stage.
9. Complete the last cl st area, throw out two pairs and sew the five remaining pairs into the starter pinloops. Tie and cut off the threads close to the lace.
10. The centre leaf requires care and accuracy when setting up. Into the centre pinloop *b* (b st), sew in two pairs of bobbins.
11. From a pin at the back of the lace, hang in another two pairs.
12. With the first two pairs, work a cl st, with two twist on each pair. Put up a pin to the right of them, in order to work the four-about-the-pin edge.
13. Cl st through one pair. Work the d st. Put up a pin. Sew into the pinloop of the leaf at *c*. Complete the edge stitch. Consult the photograph (Photo 39).
14. Cl st through one pair and work the four-about-the-pin edge. Release the pairs from the pin.
15. As the leaf progresses: a. hang in four pairs of bobbins; b. sew into the pinloops of the completed leaf; c. as the leaf narrows throw out three pairs of bobbins. Do not forget the central sewing, using the special thread; d. work the last section in h st, working the raised edge in the centre; e. as the section narrows make sewings into the leaf; f. decrease the number of pairs, until two pairs remain. Sew them into the centre pinloop at *b*. Tie and cut off the threads.

PHOTO 38 *Taurus Major*

76

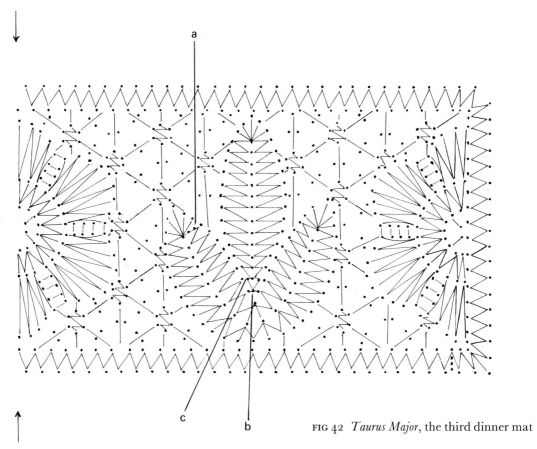

FIG 42 *Taurus Major*, the third dinner mat

PHOTO 39 Details of *Taurus Major*

77

TAURUS MINOR

Work another leaf for the corner motif.

DELPHINUS MAJOR   Linen 60/2

Techniques used in working the motif—d st edge braid, Drieblad leaf, filling no. 3, sewings into a braid, b st, false plait, h st, cl st, raised edge (straight edge), joining a braid, tying off several threads.

Method of working the motif

Make the complete pattern and prepare the pricking as described on page 107.

The outer braid
Work the outer braid as described in Cetus.

The centre of the motif
1. The first and the third leaves are set up at the centre pinhole of the leaf, using five pairs of bobbins. Three more pairs are added. Note the stitch used in each section, the b st and the tip of each leaf, where two pairs are thrown out. Firm the threads constantly.

2. The second and fourth leaves are set up by sewing in five pairs of bobbins into the pinloops and edge of the braid. The stem is worked first, finishing at the centre pin of the leaf. The second and fourth leaves are set up at the centre pin of the leaf.
3. As the leaves are worked, sewings are made into the braid.

The filling
1. Carefully work out the route for each area, taking care to work in an anti-clockwise direction.
2. Keep continuous threads for as long as possible. Each 'start and finish' is a weakness in the lace.

DELPHINUS MINOR

Work another Drieblad leaf for the corner motif.

Mounting the motifs

All the motifs are mounted on Irish linen, 26 threads per inch. 30cm × 140cm of this fabric is required to make the four dinner mats. Four-sided stitch, and hem stitching are used to complete the work. Coton Perle is used to work the four-sided stitch. 60/2 linen thread is used to work the blanket-stitch neatening, and the hem stitching.

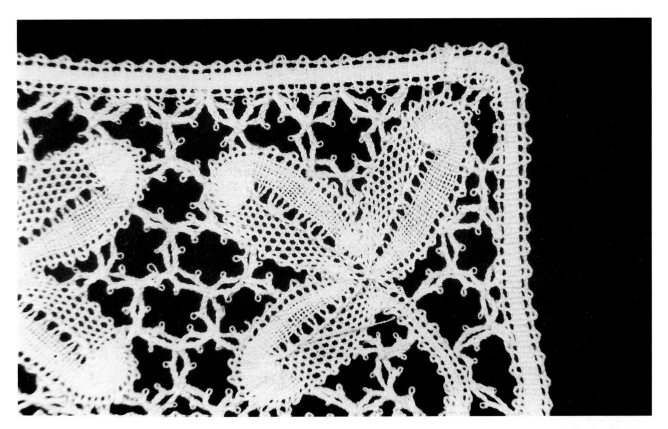

PHOTO 42 Details of *Delphinus Major*

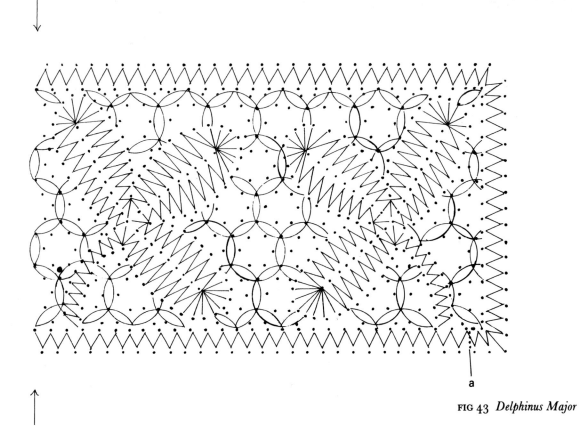

a

FIG 43 *Delphinus Major*

PHOTO 43 Another leaf shape found in Bruges Flower lace

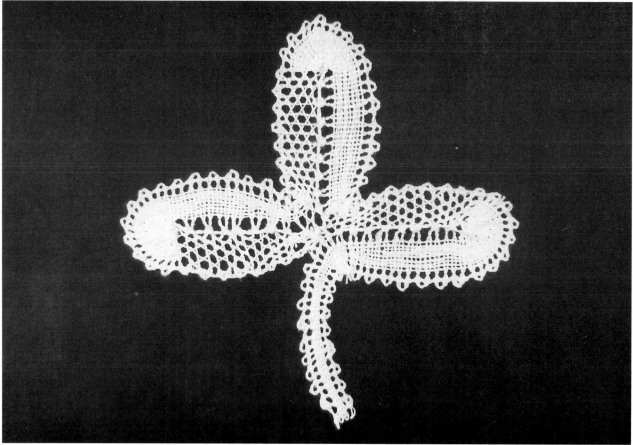

PHOTO 44 *Delphinus Minor*

1. Measure the length of the motif. The linen should be cut 2cm longer than the motif, this allows for easing the motif on to the linen, and the width required for the dinner at plus 4cm.

2. Turn over the single 2cm turning on three edges and tack this in place, mitring two corners.

3. Follow the diagrams (Figs 44 and 45) and work the four-sided stitch around the three prepared edges. Look at the photograph (Photo 35). Two or three rows of four-sided stitches may be worked through two thicknesses of fabric.

4. Consult Photo 41 and you will see that two threads, and one thread should be withdrawn along the fourth side, within the 2cm turning, the width of the braid.

5. Using blanket stitch, worked between the two rows of withdrawn threads, neaten the raw edge. Cut away the surplus fabric.

6. Tack the motif over the blanket stitch edge, to the row of the two withdrawn threads. Ease the motif on to the edge neatened with blanket stitch. Pin, tack and hemstitch the motif in position.

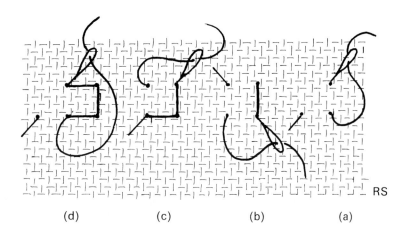

(d)   (c)   (b)   (a)

FIG 44 Stages of working four-sided stitch

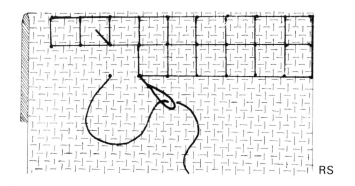

FIG 45 Two rows of four-sided stitch

FIG 46 Blanket stitch, used to neaten the raw edge

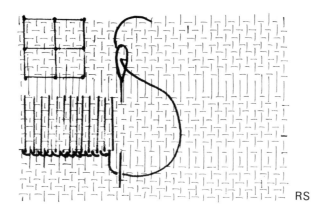

RS

FIG 47 Hem stitching, used to attach the motif to the linen
dinner mat

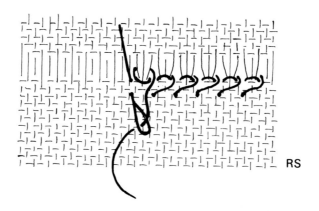

RS

RETICULUM Linen 100/2

Lacemakers aim to achieve a high standard of work to show their knowledge and skill of the craft. It may be an edging for a tablecloth, a set of dinner mats, a fan, a wedding veil, a christening robe, a wall hanging, a landscape picture, or three-dimensional lace. Fans have proved very popular, and are always searched for by collectors. I have designed a miniature fan for this book as small sticks are now available for mounting.

Techniques used in working the motif—flower no. 3, d st edge braid, b st, cl st, joining the braid, hanging in a pair, four-about-the-pin edge, sewing out a pair, sewing in a pair, tying off a number of threads, a raised edge, d st, plait-with-picot.

Method of working the motif

Make the complete pattern and prepare the pricking as described on page 107.

The outer braid
1. Along the line at *a* put up three pins. Hang on five pairs of bobbins. Follow the worker line, and using

cl st work the d st edge braid.
2. Note the b st at each corner and take care to firm the passive threads.
3. Join the braid, sewing one pair into one pinloop. Tie and cut off the threads close to the lace.

The centre of the motif
1. The flowers, are worked first. Start by working the centre flower. It should be set up by sewing five pairs of bobbins into the outer braid for the inner circle. This is worked with a raised outer edge and a d st inner edge.
2. Sew out the threads, using the pinloops and the edge of the outer braid.

The petals
A new technique is used to work the petals. Look at the photograph (Photo 45). The four pairs of passive threads remain untwisted and after each cl st, the workers are twisted once. The petals are separated by twisting each passive pair twice.
1. Working in a clockwise direction and using the

PHOTO 45 *Reticulum*, a miniature fan

FIG 48 *Reticulum*, a miniature fan

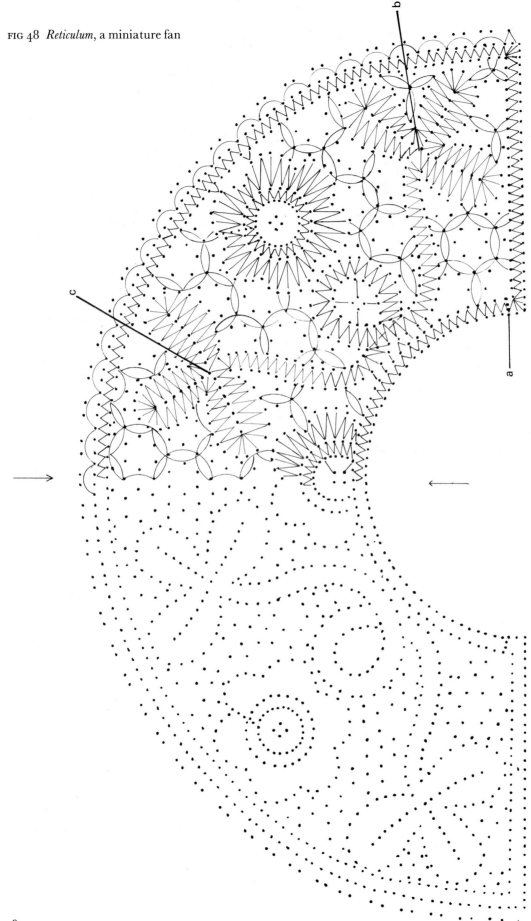

PHOTO 46 Details of the miniature fan

pinloops and the edge of the braid, sew in six pairs of bobbins.

2. Twist the four passive pairs of bobbins, twice.

3. Following the worker line, work the petals in the stitch already described. Note the sewings to make the raised edge, and firm and shape the passive threads.

4. Twist the four passive threads twice and sew them out into the outer braid. Tie and cut off the threads close to the lace.

5. Work the other flowers using the same number of bobbins and the same techniques.

The Drieblad leaves

1. Put up a pin at *b* at the centre pin and hang on six pairs of bobbins. Use the LH pair as workers, cl st to the outer edge. Work the d st edge.

2. Work back to the centre and work the four-about-the-pin edge (straight edge).

3. Continue to work the blade, hanging in four more pairs. Note the sewings into the outer braid.

4. The tip of the leaf is worked in cl st. Remember to make the sewing through the loops about the centre

pin. Throw out three pairs of bobbins ready to work the h st on the second side, and make the sewings under both of the bars to make the raised edge in the centre.

5. A turning, with b st, is made at the base of each leaf. The stitch is changed at the halfway point. Note the sewings into the outer braid.

6. Complete the leaves in this manner. Throw out one pair. Six pairs remain. Work the stem in cl st with a d st edge. Firm and shape the passive threads.

7. Note the sewings and the false plaits at the base of the stem. Cross the braids, and work the second Drieblad leaf, sewing out into the centre pinhole *c*.

8. Work the tallies in the centre of the flowers and the loop of the braid. Work the filling, remembering to keep the plaits short and firm.

The edging

Work edging no. 1.

Press the fan between two layers of damp linen until almost dry. Leave to dry naturally and catch stitch onto matching tulle.

Following the manufacturer's instructions mount onto the miniature fan sticks.

OCTANS, WEDDING VEIL   Tanne thread no. 30

The making of lace articles is now becoming an activity for groups of lacemakers. A wedding veil has been designed for a group of people to make. This design is worked in eight sections, forming a circular veil, 100cm in diameter. The design may also be used on the wedding gown for the neckline of the bodice and cuffs of the sleeve, and for the enthusiast, the gown of the dress.

The sections may be worked individually or as a continuous unit, and then mounted onto the tulle. The veil may be converted into a christening robe at a later date.

Techniques used in working the motif—flower no. 8, cl st, d st, h st, d st edge braid, raised edge sewings, leaf with h st vein, scroll, sewing.

Method of working the motif

1. Make the complete pattern, comprising two flowers, a complete braid with a scroll at each end, and half of the braid at each side of the flowers. Make a tracing of this for mounting the lace onto the tulle.
2. Prepare the pricking as described on page 107.
3. Work the flowers, using six pairs for the inner circle, and ten pairs for the petals. Look at the photograph (Photo 47) and you will see which petals are worked in cl st and which are worked in h st.
4. Now work the leaves. If a raised edge leaf is worked, sew four pairs into the flower, increasing to

PHOTO 47 *Octans*, a wedding veil

FIG 49 *Octans*, a wedding veil

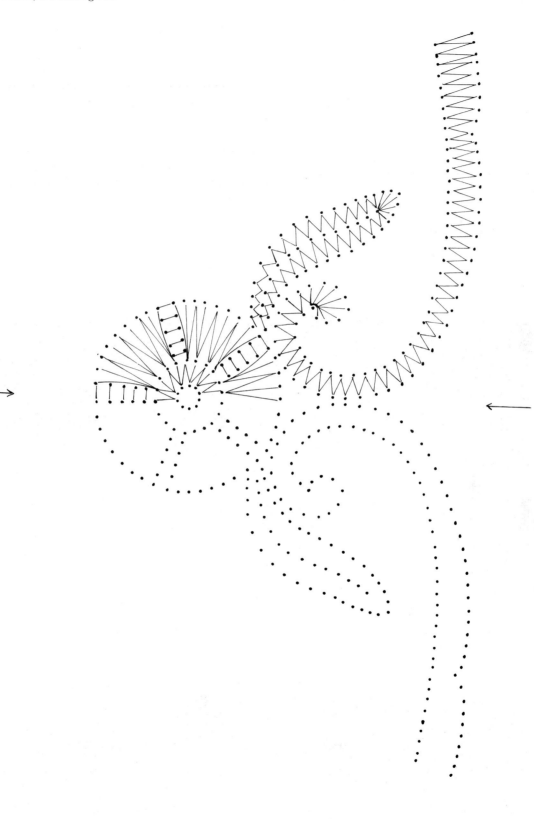

six pairs. Work the first side in cl st (throw out one pair) and the second side in h st. If a h st vein leaf is worked, start at the tip, increasing to ten pairs of bobbins. Throw out six pairs and sew out into the flower.

5. Work the scroll, increasing to eight pairs of bobbins. Sewings are made into the leaf and the flower. Notice that there are three sections of the braid: a d st edge cl st braid; a h st braid; a h st vein braid.

Each section is divided with a row of d st worked from the outer to the inner edge.

6. When working the second braid note the sewings worked into the first braid.

7. Work and join all the sections. Press all the sections between two layers of damp linen fabric. Leave to dry.

Mounting the motifs
1. Cut out a circle of tulle 110cm in diameter. Divide the tulle into eight sections with tailor tacks. Place the tulle over the tracing of the pricking, matching the motifs to the tracing.

2. Tack in position, leaving 10cm of tulle as turnings. Catch stitch the motif to the tulle between each pinloop, around each edge.

3. Cut away the surplus tulle close to the lace. Remove the tacking stitches and press between two layers of linen fabric to protect the tulle.

PHOTO 48 Details of the wedding veil

PHOTO 49 *Pollux*, a basket of flowers

FIG 50 *Pollux*, a basket of flowers

POLLUX   Tanne thread no. 30

This basket of flowers was especially designed for the book by Anne Marie Verbeke of Bruges. This design brings together many techniques of the lace and is for the experienced worker. Constant observation of the photograph will help when working this design (Photo 50). Alternative stitches may be used. The final number of bobbins used in each unit has been marked on the pattern.

Techniques used in working the motif—d st, h st, cl st, d st edge braid worked in cl st and h st, leaf plait, leaf with raised edge vein, tally, false plait, broken spider, ladder, sewings, b st, plait-with-picot.

Order of working the motif

1. Prepare the pricking as described on page 107. Note the number of pairs required to work each unit. Mark in the worker line wherever possible.
2. Start to work the LH leaf (ten prs) leading into the stem and the braid of the basket. Note the false plaits.
3. Work the four flowers observing the number of pairs used. The two joined together are described in chapter 2.
4. The plait-with-picots or leaf plaits may be worked as the lace progresses.
5. Work the leaves and the braids. Observe the number of pairs used.

   Make a note of: which stitch is to be used; how the leaf is started; the raised edge; the centre stitch used in each leaf; and the b st.
6. Finally press the lace between layers of damp linen and mount on fabric ready for framing.

PHOTO 50 Details of the basket of flowers

CEPHEI, THE CHRISTENING ROBE   Tanne
thread no. 30

The christening robe was designed for group work: a dressmaker to make up the cotton gown and the tulle over-gown; a lacemaker to work the edgings and motifs; and a needlewoman to mount the lace. The style of the gowns is simple and may be adapted from a commercial pattern. Pure cotton fabric was selected for the gown and fine nylon tulle for the over-gown. The scalloped edging can be adapted to any shaped skirt, and the simple motifs placed in any position on the lower edge. If the motifs are placed any higher, they will become lost in the folds of the tulle. The large motif is used centrally on the skirt, and on the crown of the bonnet.

Techniques used in working the motif—flower no. 2, cl st, h st, plait-with-picot, sewings, leaf with raised vein, scroll, d st edge braid.

Order of working the motif

1. Prepare the prickings as described on page 107.
2. Sketch the gown and the over-gown and mark the position of all the motifs. Make a note of the number required of each motif.
2. Eight pairs of bobbins are needed for the flowers. The plait-with-picot filling is worked as the petals progress in an anti-clockwise direction. The half flower is set up by sewing the pairs into the pinloops and the edge of the full flower.
3. Five pairs of bobbins are needed for the leaves, which have a raised central vein. The broken spider filling was used in the first section of the leaf, and cl st in the last section of the leaf.
4. Start the leaves by sewing the pairs into the pinloops and the edge of the full flower. Other

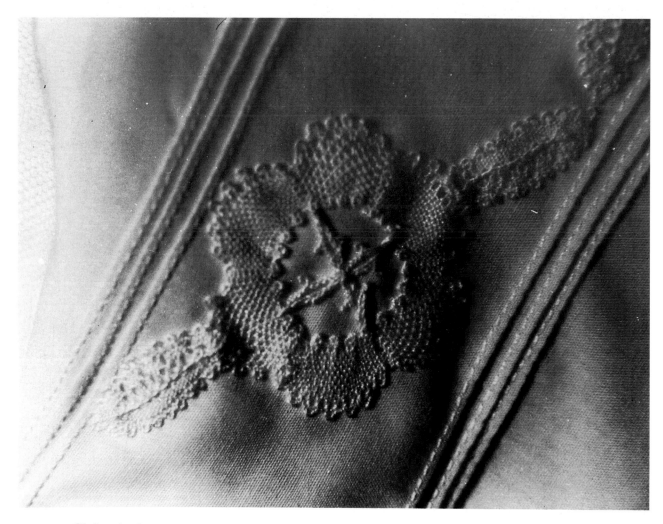

PHOTO 51 Christening bonnet

92

PHOTO 52 The small motif used on the christening robe
and the over-gown

stitches may be used with the addition of more pairs
of bobbins.

5. Work the narrow h st braids (six pairs) to neaten
the armholes and the edges of the over-gown. Work
the curved and scroll edging (six pairs) to neaten the
lower edges of the over-gown. The braid between
the scrolls is worked in cl st and h st. A row of d st
separate the two stitches.

Mounting the motifs

1. Mark the centre of the over-gown with a white
tacking thread.
2. Pin on the curved and scroll edging along the
lower edge. Pin on the h st braids at the armholes
and the edges. Ease the braid around the neck edge.

Using a white tacking thread and small stitches tack
them on.
3. Following your sketch of motifs, pin and tack
them into position.
4. Catch stitch the edges of the lace, between the
pinloops, to the tulle. A double stitch should be used
to start and finish the threads.
5. Mount the motifs on the cotton gown and the
bonnet.
6. Carefully remove the tacking threads. Press
lightly between two layers of linen.

PHOTO 53 Details of over-gown

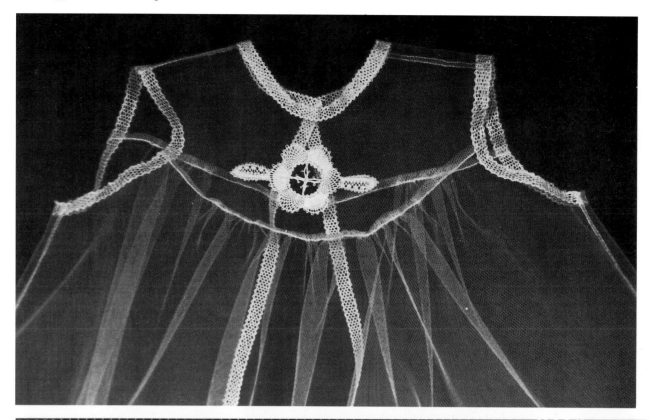

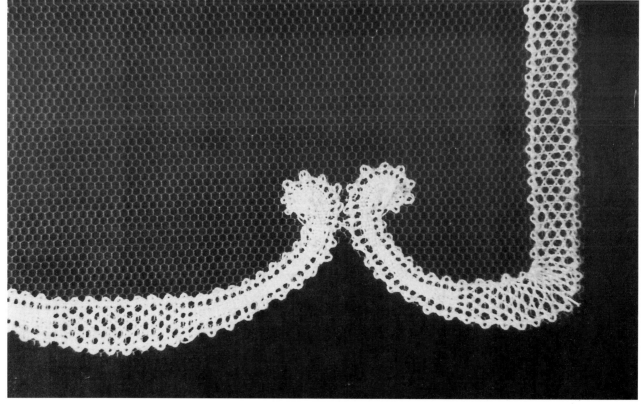

PHOTO 54 Details, showing the lower edge corners on the over-gown

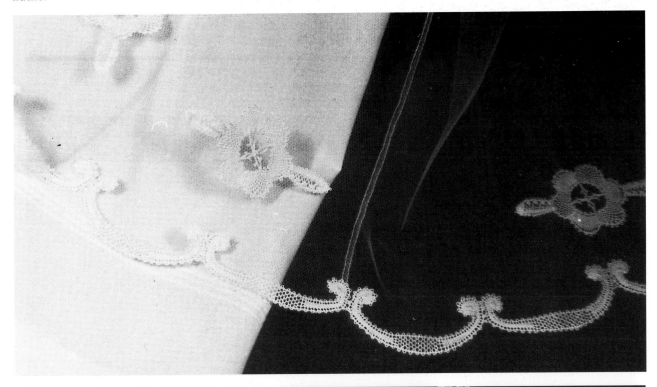

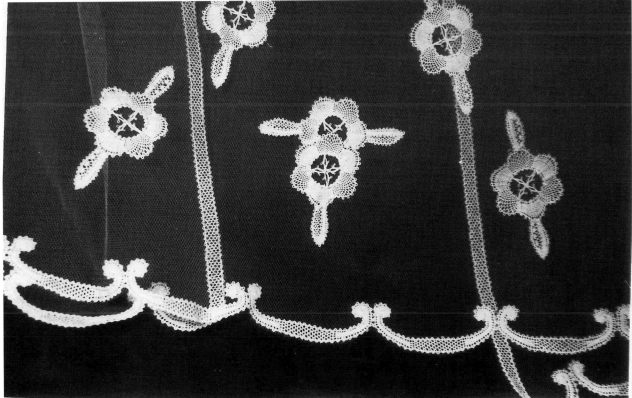

PHOTO 56 Large motif on the over-gown

PHOTO 57 Large motif used on the tulle over-gown

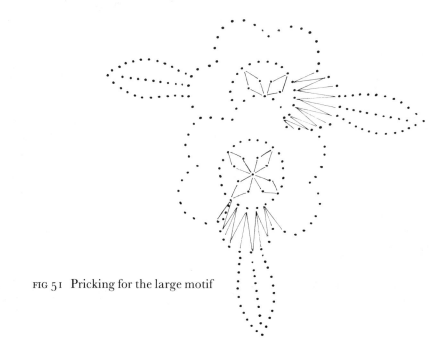

FIG 51 Pricking for the large motif

FIG 52 Pricking for the small motif

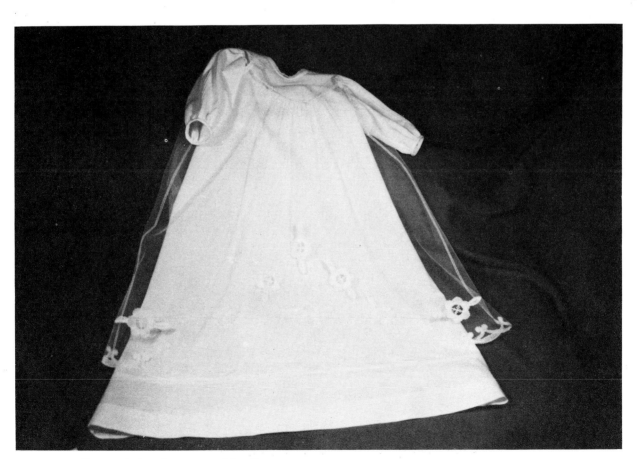

FIG 53 Pricking for the scalloped edging

PHOTO 57a Cotton christening gown with tulle over-gown

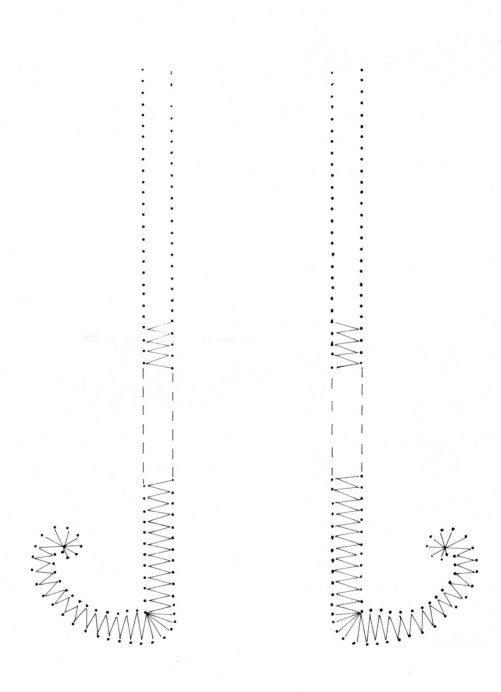

FIG 54 Pricking for corner and braid to neaten all the
edges of the tulle over-gown

PHOTO 58 Skirt of the tulle over-gown

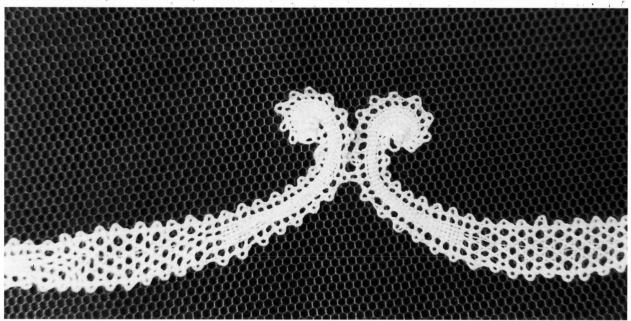

PHOTO 59 Scroll and scalloped edging tacked into position

Appendix – Explanation of basic techniques

BACK STITCH

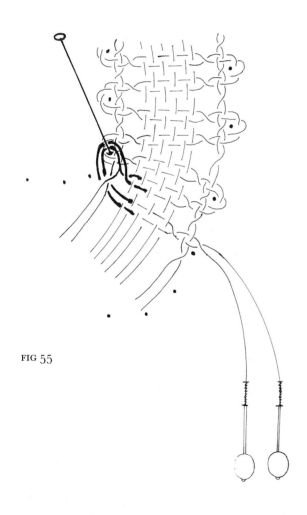

FIG 55

CROSSING THE BRAIDS

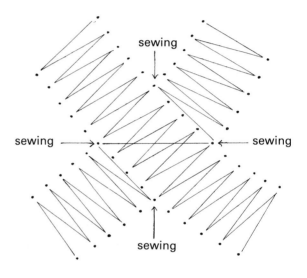

FIG 56

DIEPPE GROUND

1. Two twists on each pair.
2. H st, put up a pin.
3. Close the pin with a h st and one extra twist on each pair.

DIVIDING A BRAID

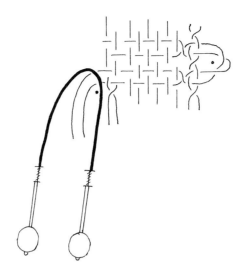

stage 1

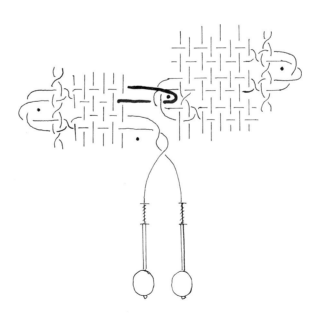

stage 2

FIG 57

EDGINGS

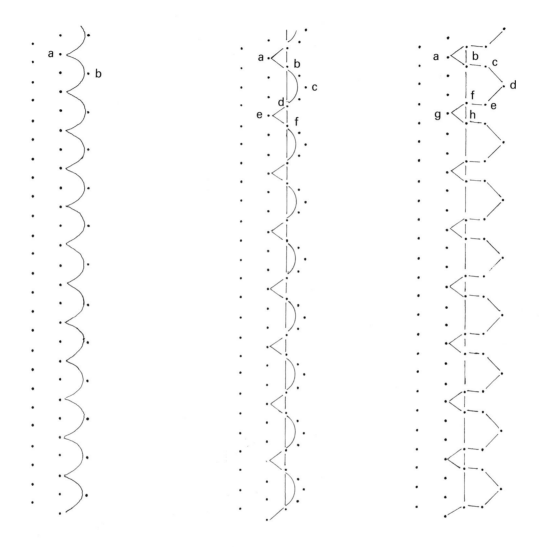

FIG 58 Edging no. 1   FIG 59 Edging no. 2   FIG 60 Edging no. 3

FALSE PLAIT

stage 1

stage 2

stage 3

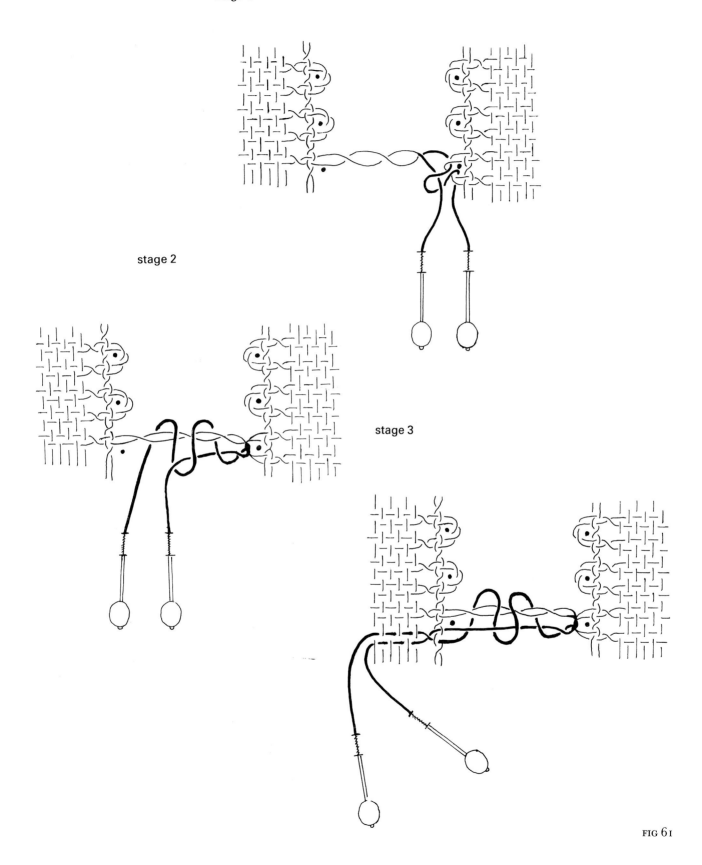

FIG 61

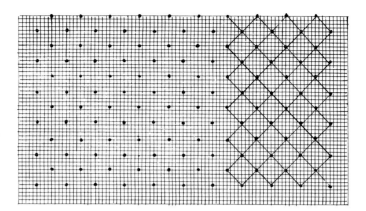

FIG 62 Filling no. 1

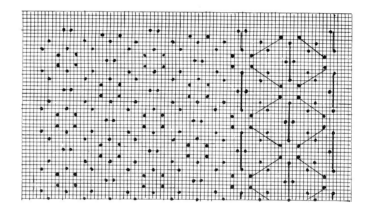

FIG 63 Filling no. 2

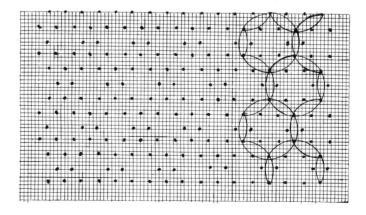

FIG 64 Filling no. 3

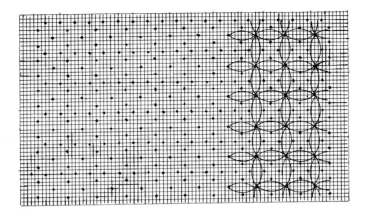

FIG 65 Filling no. 4

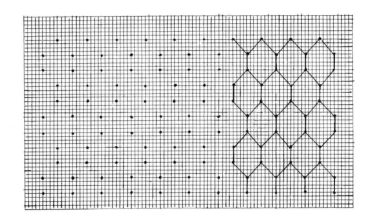

FIG 66 Filling no. 5

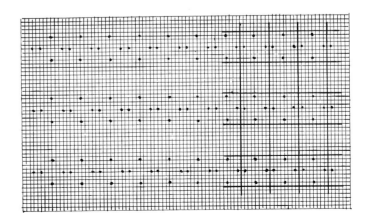

FIG 67 Filling no. 6

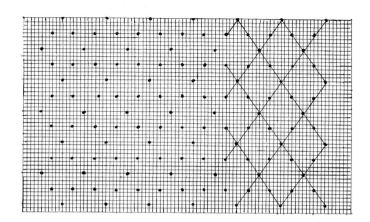

FIG 68 Filling no. 7

FINISHING A SCROLL

1. Complete the working at pin *b*, and work back to pin *a*, having thrown out the same number of threads as were hung in.

2. Take out the pin at *a*, and using the first passive pair used to make the b st, sew into the underlying three loops about the pin at *a*. The three remaining pairs should be passed through this loop.

3. Tie the loop pair firmly, and tighten all the other pairs so that the scroll is even. Open a pair which has been thrown out, lay the four pairs between these threads. Tie the four pairs down to the scroll with this pair.

4. Some of these pairs may be used to work the filling. Those not needed may be cut off close to the lace.

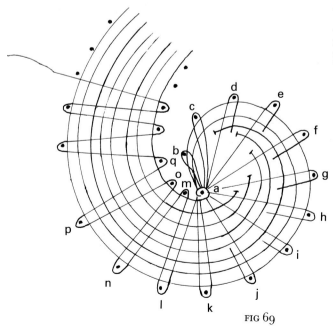

FIG 69

HANGING A PAIR INTO A BRAID

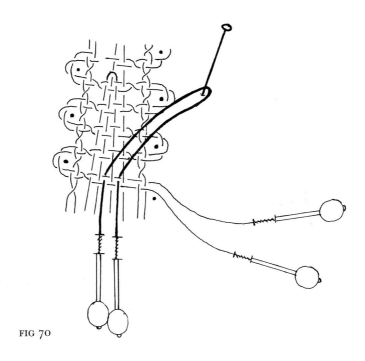

FIG 70

PREPARING THE PRICKING

1. Place the pattern on top of a piece of pricking card. Using a pricker holding a no. 9 Crewel needle, prick out the pattern. Do not miss any holes. Remove the paper pattern.
2. With a fine black felt-tipped pen copy the worker lines, b st, bars etc., from the pattern on to the card.
3. Mark the type and thickness of yarn needed on the pricking.

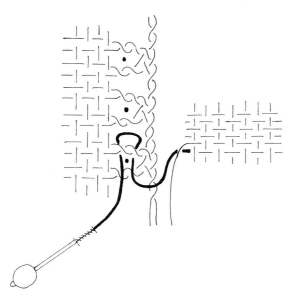

FIG 71 Raised edge sewing using one bar. Cross the worker pair to bring the passive threads closer to the raised edge

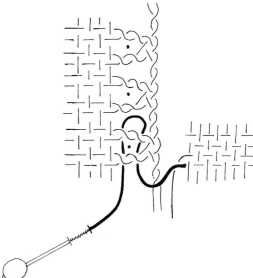

FIG 72 Raised edge sewing, using both bars

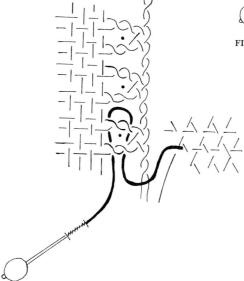

FIG 73 Raised edge sewing, half stitch, using both bars

REPLACING A THREAD

1. When a new thread is needed, introduce it by first fastening it to a pin at the back of the work. Bring the new thread beside the thread which needs replacing and twist the two threads together tightly until they resemble one thread. The two bobbins may be held together with a rubber band. Work with this double thread for about 5cm, and put the empty bobbin to the back of the work. When convenient, carefully cut off this thread and the thread from the pin close to the lace.

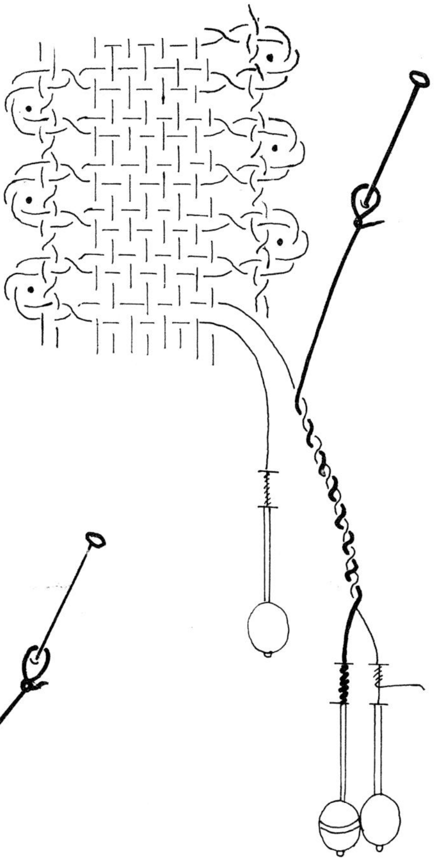

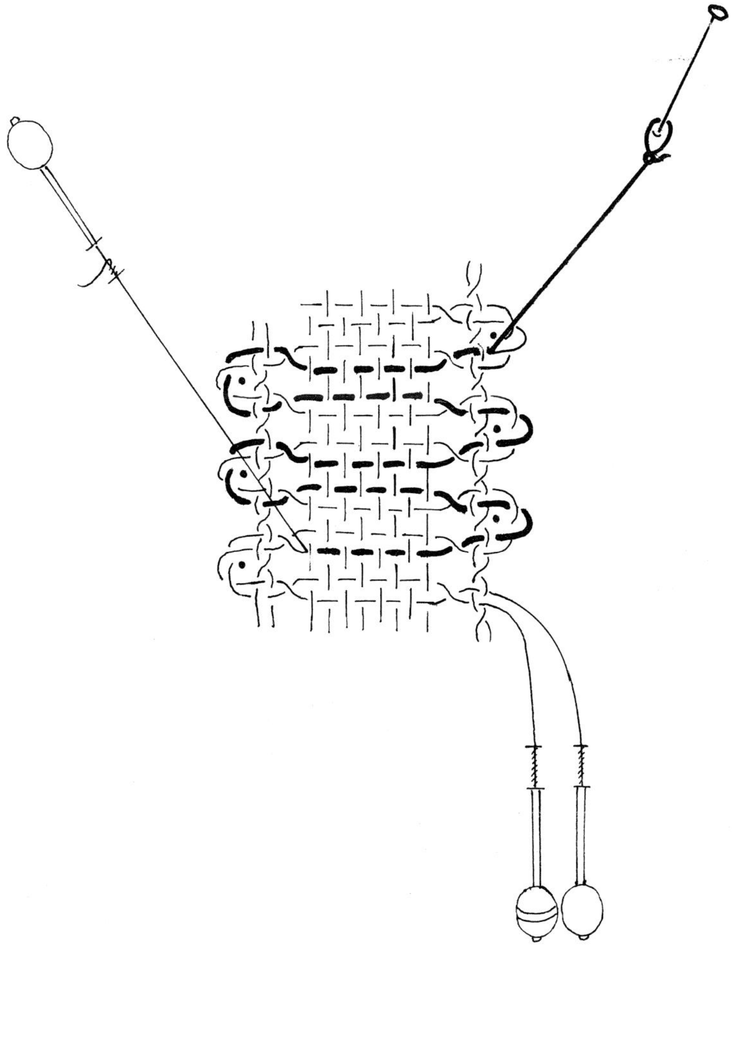

FIG 74 Replacing a thread

SETTING UP A LEAF

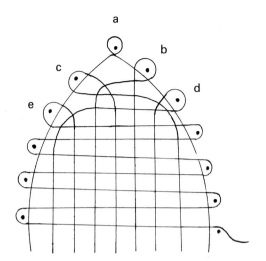

FIG 75

SETTING UP A SCROLL

1. Put up a pin at *a* and hang on four pairs of bobbins. The first pair on the left will not be used. The second pair will be the worker pair. The third pair must be twisted three times and the fourth pair twisted once.

2. Take the workers through the third pair and then work the edge stitch with the fourth pair at *b*.

3. Work back to the left through the passive pair in cl st.

4. Twist the workers twice. Lead the workers behind the pin at *a* and back under the passive pair that was left hanging.

5. The scroll will increase in width as it is worked. Pairs must now be added to accommodate the width of the scroll. Look at the diagram and you will notice where the pairs are hung in. The number of pairs added to the scroll will depend upon the thickness of the thread and the width of the scroll.

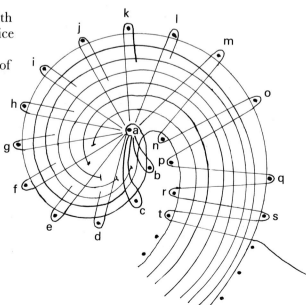

FIG 76

SEWING IN A PAIR OF BOBBINS

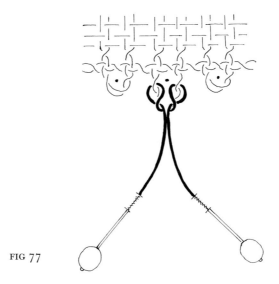

FIG 77

SEWING PAIRS INTO THE EDGE OF A
DOUBLE-STITCH BRAID

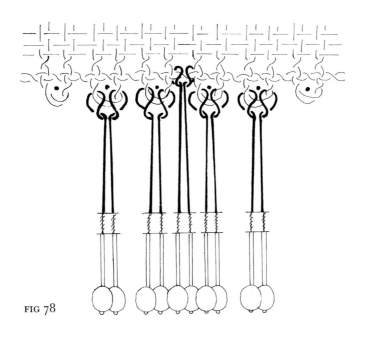

FIG 78

THROWING OUT A PAIR

1. When using cl st select two alternate threads inside the edge pairs. Lay them to the back of the work. Work two or three rows and cut off the pair which has been thrown out.
2. When using h st, select two pairs inside the first passive pair. Cross and twist them. Place the inside pair to the back, and work two or three rows of lace. Tie this pair into a reef knot and cut the threads close to the lace.

TYING OFF SEVERAL THREADS

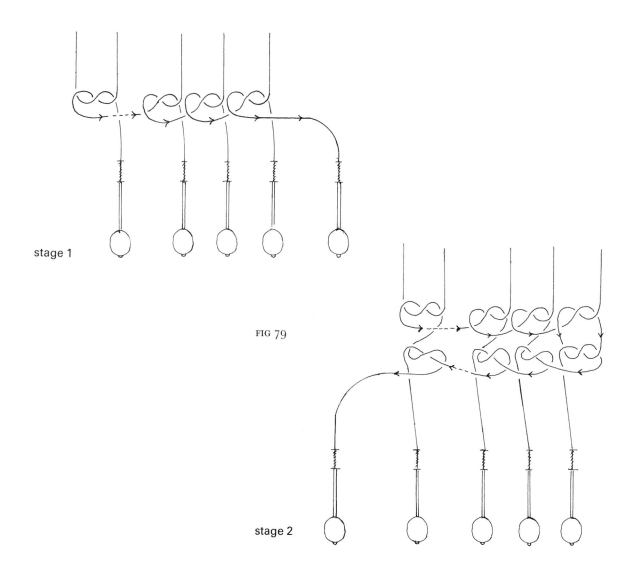

stage 1

FIG 79

stage 2

WINDMILL

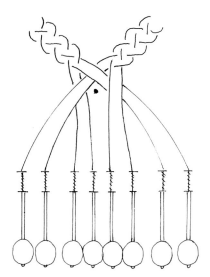

FIG 80

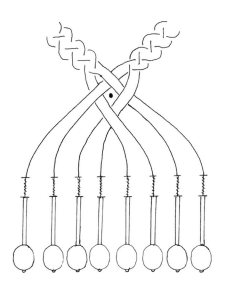

WORKING A FOUR-ABOUT-THE-PIN EDGE

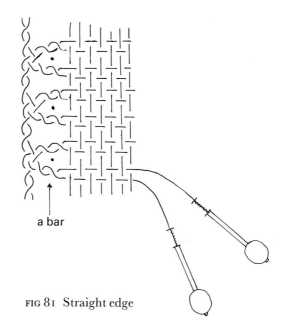

a bar

FIG 81 Straight edge

WORKING A PLAIT-WITH-PICOT

WORKING A PLAIT

1. A plait is worked with a series of h st.
2. Keep each pair to the extreme right and left and tighten the plait after each stitch.
3. There should be the same number of stitches in each plait whenever possible.

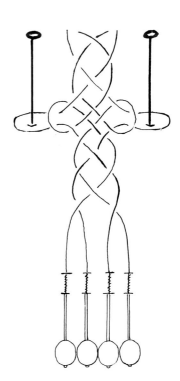

FIG 82

WORKING A SCROLL, USING A SPECIAL THREAD TO MAKE THE SEWING

1. Put up a pin and hang on the bobbins in the usual way. Look at the diagram (Fig 83).
2. Wind some of the same thread on to a pair of easily identified bobbins.
3. Hold the bobbins together and slide 'this thread' under the LH bobbins and over the RH bobbins. Secure 'this thread' (long) around a pin at the back of the work.
4. Work the scroll, top of leaf etc., and place the worker thread behind the b st pin, under 'this thread' and the b st thread.
5. When the scroll, etc., is worked, lift the loop of 'this thread'. Pass one of the b st threads through the loop. Pull 'this thread' back through all the b st. Remove 'this thread' from the loop and pass the other thread through the remaining loop.
6. Carefully reduce the loop in size and allow this pair to hang as passive threads.
7. It may be necessary to throw out another pair should the weaving appear thick and heavy.

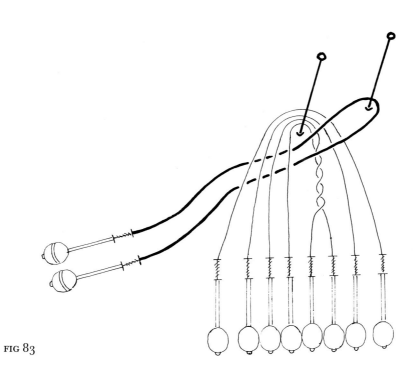

FIG 83

Index

Further reading

Channer, C. C., *Lacemaking Point Ground*, Dryad Press Ltd

Claire, Raie, *The Dryad Book of Bobbin Lace*, Dryad Press Ltd

d'Arcy, Eithne, *Irish Crochet Lace*, Dryad Press Ltd

Dye, Gilian, *Beginning Bobbin Lace*, Dryad Press Ltd

Fisher, Jennifer, *Braid Lace for Today*, Dryad Press Ltd

Fisher, Jennifer, *Torchon Lace for Today*, Dryad Press Ltd

Hardeman, Henk, *Torchon Patterns*, Dryad Press Ltd

Harris, Valerie, *The Lavendon Collection of Bobbin Lace Patterns*, Dryad Press Ltd

Jones, Rebecca, *Complete Book of Tatting*, Dryad Press Ltd

Konior, Mary, *A Pattern Book of Tatting*, Dryad Press Ltd

Lewis, Robin, *101 Torchon Patterns*, Dryad Press Ltd

Lovesey, Nenia, and Barley, Catherine, *Venetian Gros Point Lace*, Dryad Press Ltd

O'Cleirigh, Nellie, *Carrickmacross Lace*, Dryad Press Ltd

O'Conner, Eileen, *Irish Lace Making*, Dryad Press Ltd

Stillwell, Alexandra, *Drafting Torchon Lace Patterns*, Dryad Press Ltd

Sutton, Edna, *Bruges Flower Lace*, Dryad Press Ltd

Withers, Jean, *Mounting and Using Lace*, Dryad Press Ltd

York, Sheila, *Projects in Tatting*, Dryad Press Ltd

Dryad Press Lace Books

Gillian Dye, *Beginning Bobbin Lace*, £7.50

Jennifer Fisher, *Braid Lace for Today*, £8.95.

Edna Sutton, *Bruges Flower Lace*, £8.50

Neilli O'Cleirigh, *Carrickmacross Lace*, £6.50

Ros Hills, *Colour and Texture in Needlelace*, £8.95

Levá-Skrovánová/Stan Skoumal, *Contemporary Bohemian Lace*, £8.50

Valerie Paton, *Creative Lace Patterns*, £8.95

Edna Sutton, *Designing for Bruges Flower Lace*, £8.95

Alexandra Stillwell, *Drafting Torchon Lace Patterns*, £8.95

Raie Clare, *Dryad Book of Bobbin Lace*, £9.95

Doreen Holmes, *Flowers in Needlepoint Lace*, £8.95

Eithne D'Arcy, *Irish Crochet Lace*, £6.50

Eileen O'Connor, *Irish Lace Making*, £4.95

C. C. Channer & M. Waller, *Lacemaking Point Ground*, £4.95

Valerie Harris, *Lavendon Collection of Bobbin Lace*, £9.95

Veronica Rowe, *Limerick Lace*, £6.50

Jean Withers, *Mounting and Using Lace*, £8.50

Edna Groves, *A New Approach to Embroidered Net*, £8.50

Elwyn Kenn, *Point Ground Patterns from Australia*, £4.95

Nenia Lovesey, *Punto Tagliato Lace*, £8.95

Jennifer Fisher, *Torchon Lace for Today*, £8.95

Nenia Lovesey & Catherine Barley, *Venetian Gros Point Lace*, £8.95

For further details on all Dryad Press craft titles please write to:

Dryad Press Limited
8 Cavendish Square
London W1M 0AJ

B T Batsford Lace Books

Tessa Lorant, *Batsford Book of Hand & Machine Knitted Laces*, £7.50

Pamela Nottingham, *The Batsford Lace Pattern Pack: Bucks Point*, £4.99

Elsie Luxton, *Batsford Lace Pattern Pack: Honiton*, £4.99

Pat Earnshaw, *Bobbin & Needle Laces: Identification & Care*, £12.95

Gillian Dye, *Bobbin Lace Braid*, £10.95

Cynthia Voysey, *Bobbin Lace in Photographs*, £14.95

Pamela Nottingham, *Bobbin Lace Making*, hardback £9.95, paperback £5.95

Tiny Zwaal-Line, *Bobbin Lace Patterns*, £9.95

Bridget M. Cook & Geraldine Stott, *Book of Bobbin Lace Stitches*, £12.95

Pamela Nottingham, *Bucks Point Lacemaking*, £9.95

Henk Hardeman, *Bucks Point Lace Patterns (with Tear-Out Prickings)*, £9.95

Ann Collier, *Creative Design in Bobbin Lace*, £10.95

Nenia Lovesey, *Creative Design in Needlepoint Lace*, £10.95

Elsie Luxton, *Honiton Lace Patterns*, £10.95

Bridget Cook, *Introduction to Bobbin Lace Patterns*, £9.95

Bridget M. Cook & Geraldine Stott, *Introduction to Bobbin Lace Stitches*, £9.95

Susanne Thompson, *Introduction to Honiton Lace*, £9.95

Nenia Lovesey, *Introduction to Needlepoint Lace*, £9.95

Alice-May Bullock, *Lace & Lacemaking*, £10.95

Pat Earnshaw, *Lace in Fashion*, £12.95

Pat Earnshaw, *Lace Machines and Machine Laces*, £19.95

Margaret Maidment, *Manual of Hand-Made Bobbin Lacework*, £10.95

Veronica Sorenson, *Modern Lace Designs*, £10.95

Cynthia Voysey, *Needlelace in Photographs*, £14.95

Tiny Zwaal-Lint, *New Bobbin Lace Patterns*, £9.95

Jane Atkinson, *Pattern Design for Torchon Lace*, £10.95

Bridget M. Cook, *Practical Skills in Bobbin Lace*, £14.95

Pat Parryman & Cynthia Voysey, *New Designs in Honiton Lace*, £9.95

Ann Collier, *New Designs in Bobbin Lace*, £11.95

Elizabeth Prickett, *Ruskin Lace and Linen Work*, £9.95

Pamela Nottingham, *Technique of Bobbin Lace*, £12.95

Pamela Nottingham, *Technique of Bucks Point Lace, Technique of Crocheted & Openwork Lace*, £10.95

Pauline Knight, *Technique of Filet Lace*, £10.95

Geraldine Stott & Bridget M. Cook, *100 Traditional Bobbin Lace Patterns*, £12.95

Elsie Luxton, *Technique of Honiton Lace*, £10.95

Ena Maidens, *Technique of Irish Crochet Lace*, £12.95

Nenia Lovesey, *Technique of Needlepoint Lace*, £10.95

Alexandra Stillwell, *Technique of Teneriffe Lace*, £10.95

Pamela Nottingham, *Technique of Torchon Lace*, £10.95

Henk Hardeman, *Torchon lace Patterns*, £9.95

Geraldine Stott, *A Visual Introduction to Bucks Point Lace*, £10.95

For further details on all B T Batsford craft titles please write to:

B T Batsford Limited
4 Fitzhardinge Street
London W1H 0AH

Suppliers

European

Cibeles B V
Vijverlaan 497
2925 VH Krimpen aan den Ijssel
The Netherlands

Scharlacken
Philipstockstraat 5 & 7
B 8000 Brugge
Belgium

't handwerkhuisje
Katelijnestraat 23
8000 Brugge
Belgium

't Vlaskeldertje
St Annastraat 189
6525 GM
Nijmegen
The Netherlands

UK

Alby Lace Centre
Cromer Road
Alby
Norwich
Norfolk

English Lace School
Honiton Court
Rockbeare
Nr Exeter
Devon

Frank Herring & Sons
27 High West Street
Dorchester
DT1 1UP

Honiton Lace Shop
44 High Street
Honiton
Devon

D. J. Hornsby
149 High Street
Burton Latimer
Kettering
Northants

Enid Taylor
Valley House Craft Studio
Ruston
Scarborough
N. Yorks
YO13 9QE

Hepatica
82A Water Lane
Wilmslow
Cheshire

The Lace Guild
c/o The Hollies
53 Audnam
Stourbridge
West Midlands
DY8 4AE

Mace and Nairn
89 Crane Street
Salisbury
Wilts

B. Phillips
Pantglas
Cellah
Lampeter
Dyfed

Sebalace
76 Main Street
Addingham
Ilkley
West Yorks
LS29 0PL

A. Sells
Lane Cove
49 Pedley Lane
Clifton
Shefford
Beds

D. H. Shaw
47 Zamar Crescent
Thurscroft
Rotherham
S. Yorks

C. & D. Springett
21 Hillmorton Road
Rugby
Warwicks
CV22 5BE

George White
Delaheys Cottage
Thistle Hill
Knaresborough
N. Yorks

Capt. J. R. Howell
19 Summerwood Lane
Halsall
Nr Ormskirk
Lancs
L39 8RG

Grids used for Lace Pattern Drafting

1. 5 mm squares

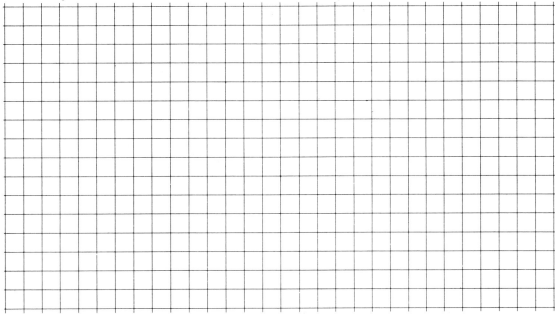

2. 6 squares = 25 mm (4 mm squares)

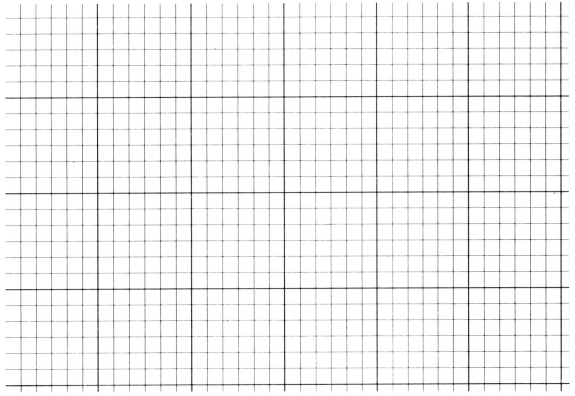

3. 8 squares = 25 mm (use 2 squares to give 4 sq. = 25 mm)

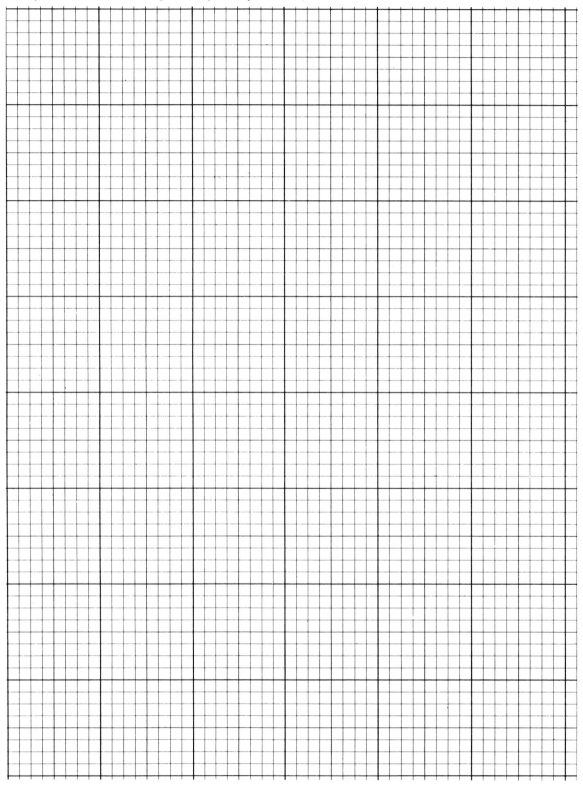

4. 10 squares = 25 mm

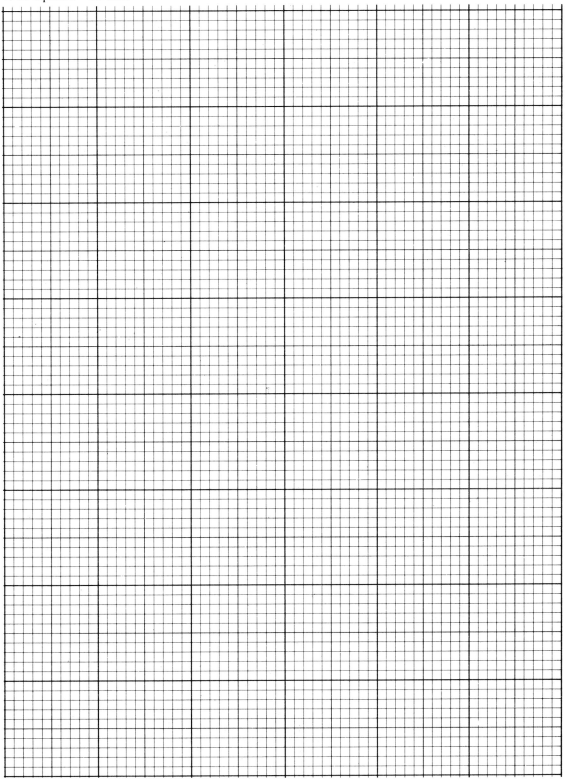

5. 2 mm squares

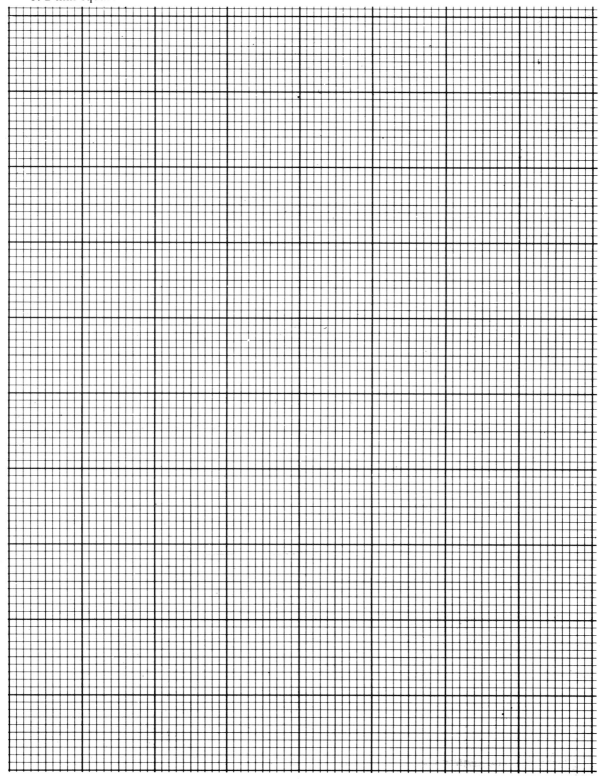